EXPLORING THE
Wild
Oregon Coast

EXPLORING THE
Wild Oregon Coast

BONNIE HENDERSON

THE
MOUNTAINEERS

Published by
The Mountaineers
1001 SW Klickitat Way
Seattle, Washington 98134

Published simultaneously in Canada by Douglas & McIntyre, Ltd., 1615 Venables Street, Vancouver, B.C. V5L 2H1

First edition: first printing 1994, second printing 1997

Manufactured in the United States of America

Edited by Linda Gunnarson
Maps by Debbie Newell
All photographs by Bonnie Henderson, except the following:
    Michael S. Thompson, cover, pages 2–3, 10, 17, 37, 41, 45, 53, 69, 72, 73, 79, 89, 96, 99, 132, 146, 150, 155, 161, 175, 181, 184, 188, 190, 199, 209, 225;
    Bob and Ira Spring, pages 43, 57, 93, 126, 135, 176, 194, 197;
    David Vanderlip, page 239
Book layout and typesetting by The Mountaineers Books

Cover photograph: Hiking in Boardman State Park
Frontispiece: View from Boardman State Park

Library of Congress Cataloging in Publication Data
Henderson, Bonnie.
        Exploring the wild Oregon coast / Bonnie Henderson.
            p.   cm.
        Includes index.
        ISBN 0-89886-358-9
            1. Outdoor recreation—Oregon—Guidebooks. 2. Oregon Coast Trail—Guidebooks. 3. Oregon—Guidebooks. I. Title.
GV191.42.O2H47   1993
796.5'09795--dc20
                                                        93-44840
                                                        CIP

For today's and tomorrow's children,
but especially for John

Contents

Key to Map Symbols

—(101)—	U.S. Highway
—(53)—	State Highway
———	Secondary Road
■■■■■■■	Gravel Road
----------	Trail
···············	Hiking Route (on road)
···············	Hiking Route (on beach)
- - - - - - -	Hiking Route (on trail)
Ⓣ	Trailhead
▲	Mountain Summit
∴	Sand
~	River/Stream
⚘	Marsh
⛴	Boat Launch
⛴	Ferry
⊼	Picnic Area
▲	Campground
↟	Restroom
✶	Windmill
↯	Viewpoint
☗	Lighthouse
▬ ·· ▬	State Boundary
▬ · ▬ ·	Park Boundary

8

Acknowledgments

*M*any thanks...
- To my family for their constant encouragement and enthusiasm.
- To the friends who accompanied me on hikes in rain and shine, including Sue, Gil, and Dad.
- To my Cannon Beach family—Betsy, Gary, Meadow, and Cory—for shelter, shuttles, support, trail companionship, and love.
- To staff at the University of Oregon Map Library, especially those charged with reshelving the topographical maps.
- To the many professionals at the U.S. Fish and Wildlife Service, Oregon Department of Fish and Wildlife, U.S. Forest Service, Bureau of Land Management, Oregon State Parks and Recreation Department, Oregon State University, Hatfield Marine Science Center, various county offices, and other universities and public agencies that shared their knowledge and offered valuable guidance, or reviewed the manuscript for accuracy. Among them: Pete Bond, Debra Brosnan, Judy Chamberlain, Jim Chambers, Julie Cox, Don Giles, Steve Gobat, Katie Grenier, Mike Hewitt, Don Higginson, Roger Holstein, Don Howard, Sabrina Keen, Ed Kornblum, Andy LaTomme, Roy Lowe, Bev Lund, Gene Large, Kim Nelson, Claire Puchy, Steven Rumrill, Charlie Severson, Kate Stafford, George Taylor, Rick Taylor, Richard Walkoski, Kathy Jo Wall, Cheryl Walters, and Megan Yeary.
- To the many people I met along the way who freely shared their expertise and enthusiasm and even gave me lifts, and who generally made my day again and again.
- To the staff at The Mountaineers Books, for their patience.

Introduction

For nearly 400 scenic miles US 101 winds down the Oregon coast, passing through towns and hamlets full of motels and shops, offering dazzling ocean views from the car window. This book isn't about US 101, however. It's about getting off US 101 and onto the wild Oregon coast, a realm of primeval forests and undulating sand dunes, secret beaches and towering headlands, of elk and eagles and hermit crabs scuttling across tide-filled rock pools.

In 1967 Oregon's landmark Beach Bill was signed into law, granting the public access to all of the state's beaches—not only to the high-tide line but all the way to the vegetation line. The law formalized a tradition first established by coastal Indians and continued by the earliest white settlers, who gathered food on the beaches and used them as their primary north-south highway. Construction of US 101 moved most purposeful travel off the beach, allowing it to become a place to contemplate and play, to stretch muscles and imagination, a place where curiosity about wild things is piqued and sometimes satisfied, and creativity (and the family dog) can run free.

The beach isn't the only feature of the Oregon coast that's still wild, however, thanks in part to vigorous efforts to preserve adjacent shore and forest lands and to develop trails and other recreational facilities. There are trails over headlands and along estuaries, some leading to hidden beaches or deep into old-growth Sitka spruce forests; exceptional tidepools protected as marine gardens; secluded lake fingers and estuaries ideal for canoeing; interpretive centers ranging from the elegantly simple South Slough National Estuarine Sanctuary visitors' center to the dazzling Oregon Coast Aquarium. Linking it all is a border-to-border coastal hiking trail, unique in the country. With its relatively mild weather, the coast is accessible to hikers virtually year-round, long after snow has closed Cascade trails, and it's as close or closer to those dwelling in Oregon's western valleys as are the mountain trails to the east.

This book is a comprehensive guide to nonmotorized recreational opportunities on Oregon's shoreline and adjacent public

Opposite: Whalehead Beach in Boardman State Park

lands. Though it covers the entire 362-mile coastline, its scope is limited to the beaches and public lands just inland, contiguous with US 101. Many more intriguing recreational opportunities exist in the western foothills of the Coast Range and Siskiyous, but other books (such as The Mountaineers' *50 Hikes in Oregon's Coast Range and Siskiyous*) cover those areas quite well. Where irresistible, brief mention is made of a few such opportunities in the appropriate chapters.

Bear in mind that the trails on the Oregon coast are, generally speaking, not wilderness trails. Some feel quite remote and aren't particularly well traveled, granting hikers a good degree of solitude. Others are popular, even crowded on summer weekends. But part of what's so appealing about the Oregon coast is its variety. It's quite easy in summer to find a popular beach abuzz with vacation energy: kites are flying, beach fires are burning, and children are building sand castles. It's really just as easy, if you know where to go, to find a very remote beach, where there are few if any other people with whom to share miles of open sand or an orange-and-rose sunset. This book is designed to help you choose the kind of coastal experience you want.

How to Use This Book

This book describes recreational opportunities on the Oregon coast by dividing the coast into twenty-five roughly equal-size sections and dedicating a chapter to each. Chapters are arranged geographically, north to south, corresponding to the natural direction a summertime beach walker would go to keep the wind at her back. Within each section, opportunities for beach walking, trail hiking, tidepooling, and canoeing are described, with occasional discussions of horseback riding, mountain biking, and family cycling as well. All state park campgrounds, plus some other public campgrounds of note, are mentioned where appropriate.

If you're traveling on a particular part of the coast, turn to that section and read about what's available in the way of outdoor recreation. Alternately, if you're planning a trip to the coast and are trying to decide where to go, scan various chapters, concentrating on the activities that most interest you. Nearly every chapter describes opportunities to hike and beach walk; to help you locate information in this book regarding interpretive centers, off-highway cycling, tidepool areas, wildlife watching, canoe or kayak put-ins, and horse camps and trails scattered along the coast, see Appendix II.

Not all beach access points are mentioned in this book, nor do

Log creek-crossing on trail to south end of Threemile Lake

they all appear on the maps accompanying the text. The Oregon State Parks and Recreation Department has developed a plethora of waysides and other public beach access points; most are easy to find via signs posted on US 101.

Businesses open and close, owners change, and so do phone numbers. For that reason, few telephone numbers of private businesses are given, and most of the facilities mentioned are those in public ownership (in most cases run by the Forest Service or the Oregon State Parks and Recreation Department). There is a listing of telephone numbers for relevant visitor centers, ranger stations, state parks, and interpretive centers in Appendix I.

Discussions of canoeing and kayaking opportunities are oriented toward people traveling with their own boats, though rental boats may be available in the area. Similarly, discussions of horseback-riding opportunities are limited to trails and to campgrounds that cater to horse owners. Opportunities for trail riding with an outfitter are available in several locations along the coast, however. Check with chambers of commerce for information about boat or bike rentals or guided horseback riding; most horse outfitters make themselves easy to find with signs along US 101.

Trail Descriptions. Within each chapter, general information about hiking opportunities is given, with suggestions offered for creating one-way or loop hikes. These are followed by specific mile-by-mile trail descriptions of individual trails. Each begins with the trail's one-way distance (if it is a loop trail, it is so specified); be sure to double the mileage if you're planning an out-and-back hike.

Elevation gain refers to the approximate number of feet you'll ascend one way, hiking the trail from the main trailhead. (On some trails, you may descend that distance before ascending on the return.) If the elevation gain is less than about 100 feet, as is often the case on shoreline trails, no figure is given. The purpose of listing elevation change is to give readers a concrete idea of how taxing the hike will be: for example, whether it's an easy, relatively level walk or a 1,000-foot headland ascent.

Trails with trailheads at both ends are generally described north to south, unless access is clearly better at the south end. Each trail description includes driving directions from US 101, either within the trail description or in the preceding narrative describing hiking opportunities in the immediate area.

Maps. The book's chapters are grouped into five geographical regions, each with a map showing main towns and points of interest. In addition, nearly every trail description is accompanied by a map

View south from Blacklock Point

showing road access, trailhead locations, and the trail route. Some maps indicate the location of canoe or kayak launch sites mentioned in the text as well. If you're planning to hike well-maintained trails (like most of the trails in this book) in daylight and don't plan to do any cross-country exploration, the maps in this book should suffice for a day hike. For anything more extensive, a topographical map and compass are recommended. For the north-central, central, and south-central coast, a Siuslaw National Forest map showing all roads and public campground locations and most trailheads along the shore and in the Coast Range is helpful; likewise a Siskiyou National Forest map for the south coast. The Oregon Dunes National Recreation Area has an even more detailed map available for the south-central coast, from Florence to Coos Bay.

Oregon Coast Trail. A special section at the back of the book serves as a guide to the Oregon Coast Trail (OCT), a 400-mile border-to-border trail still being developed along the coast. Refer to this section if you're interested in a multiday backpacking trip, or a long or varied day hike incorporating forest and beach, or perhaps a trip to a remote sand spit that includes a river-mouth boat shuttle.

Beach Safety

Weather, waves, tides, and the landforms they create produce particular hazards for those exploring the coastal environment. Take precautions to avoid getting into trouble with the following common coastal dangers.

Sneaker, or Rogue, Waves. In summer, waves tend to roll onto the beach with fairly predictable force and rhythm. In winter, particularly during or just after a storm, unusually large waves frequently roll onto the beach, easily knocking down anyone in their path. Every winter on the Oregon coast at least one or two deaths are attributed to such sneaker waves. If you're knocked down near where a creek is emptying into the ocean, it's that much more difficult to drag yourself out of the surf. The moral: don't turn your back to the ocean, and be particularly careful to keep yourself and your children well above the waves during winter beach walks.

Drifting Logs. Winter storms carry fallen logs down coastal rivers to the sea, where they may wash in the surf until they're stranded on the sand. Stay away from any logs at or near the water's edge; if a wave should slip beneath one and cause it to start floating, it could easily crush you if you fall beneath it.

Cliff and Headland Climbing. Not only does free climbing on steep cliff faces pose obvious, inherent risks, but much of the rock at the shore is crumbly sandstone, which only increases the danger of falling. Some popular trails follow right along the tops of steep seaside cliffs—safe only if you stick to the trail. Take informal spur trails leading from marked trails down to hidden beaches or coves at your own risk. Walk out onto jetties only with great caution. It may look (and be) safe at low tide, but when the tide rises, large waves may wash onto the jetty, particularly during storms.

Rip Currents (Undertows). If the Pacific Ocean along Oregon weren't an uninviting 47 to 52 degrees Fahrenheit, even more swimmers would be caught by rip currents along the coast. The danger is twofold: a swimmer fighting a rip current may be unable to swim to shore and may drown, or may perish from hypothermia simply from excessive exposure to the cold water. If you do get caught in a current that's pulling you away from the shore, don't try to swim against it directly. It's best to work at staying afloat in a horizontal position and staying calm. Swim or drift parallel to the shore until you get out of the current; then swim in to shore at a different spot. **Tide Dangers.** Algae can make rocks in tidepool areas extremely slippery. Even if the rock is dry, you'll still slip if your shoes' soles are wet. Wear boots or athletic shoes with a gripping sole and begin exploring cautiously, noting which kinds of rocks are slipperiest. Watch the time and the water level as well, to make sure you don't get stranded on a rock by an incoming tide. Likewise, watch the time and your tide table if you're rounding a headland so that you don't get stranded between an incoming tide and a sheer cliff face. **Falling Trees.** Only the most paranoid hiker would worry about a tree falling on him while he's traipsing along a forest trail—unless he happens to be out in one of the coast's ferocious winter sou'westers. With proper rain gear it can be an exciting time to be out, but occasionally people *are* killed by trees falling in such weather. Stay off headland trails during winter storms.

Beach Etiquette

Beach Fires. Unlike California, Oregon allows fires on the beach. The only restriction: beach fires must not be built in the middle of a large pile of driftwood, which might burn long after your hot dog has been roasted and you've gone home. Using individual pieces of driftwood collected on the beach is acceptable, however. Don't build fires near dune grass or other vegetation. And when you're ready to leave, douse your fire with water or wet sand to keep it from burning indefinitely. **Tidepool Exploration.** It's virtually impossible to peek into tidepools without disturbing their

Gull surveying dunes near Ophir State Wayside

17

residents and thereby degrading the very environment you've come to explore. It helps, however, if you walk only, or mostly, on bare rocks, rather than on those rocks covered with barnacles, mussels, or other animals or plants, or in the pools themselves. Refrain from picking up or even touching any animals or plants from intertidal areas (collection is prohibited or restricted at several state-designated "marine gardens"). Most of all, explore the intertidal zone slowly, for your own enjoyment and for the benefit of the creatures that live there. For additional suggestions, see Chapter 10.

Offshore Rocks. Nearly all of Oregon's more than 1,400 offshore rocks, reefs, and islands are protected as wildlife refuges (see Chapter 25). Some of those rocks are easily accessible on foot, especially at low tide. It may be tempting, but don't climb them. Because disturbance by humans easily upsets nesting birds, no trespassing is allowed on federally protected rocks. Anyone caught walking or climbing in a protected area may be fined.

Camping

In addition to the many motels, condominiums, and B&Bs along the coast, there are hundreds of campgrounds, both public and private. Among the public campgrounds, the seventeen run by state parks are among the most comfortable, with hot and cold water, showers, and facilities for motor homes. All are open from mid-April through September; nine are open year-round. Oswald West State Park on the north coast offers primitive hike-in camping (and provides wheelbarrows to help visitors transport their gear); all the rest have drive-in sites with full hookups available, as well as simple tent sites for those arriving by foot or bike. Reservations are available at nine coastal state park campgrounds in summer. Since they tend to fill up nearly every summer weekend, it's wise to make advance reservations. To do so, call 800-452-5687 from anywhere in Oregon except Portland, or 503-238-7488 in Portland or from out of state for information. The telephone numbers for the nine individual campgrounds that take reservations in summer are listed in Appendix I.

The twenty National Forest campgrounds on the coast are relatively primitive; most have no hot water or hookups. And most, including those in the Oregon Dunes National Recreation Area, are on the central coast. They're cheaper than state park campgrounds, and usually they don't fill up as fast. Note that Sand Beach Campground, southwest of Tillamook, and campgrounds located near dune buggy staging areas in the Oregon dunes tend to be dominated by noisy ORVs. Some National Forest campgrounds take reservations in summer; call Mistix at 800-280-2267.

County park campgrounds range from very spartan to full-service; Windy Cove at Winchester Bay even has cable TV. Fees vary. Only one, Barview in Tillamook County, currently accepts reservations; call 503-322-3522.

In addition there are dozens of private campgrounds, most of them easy to find from US 101. Though they cater primarily to RVs, tent campers might give them a try as well; some have delightful view sites, or at least wind-fenced niches for tent campers, with hot showers to boot. Fees run about the same as those at state parks.

Suggestions for Hikers

What to Take. Carry the same gear you would on any day hiking or backpacking trip, with a few modifications. You certainly don't need to worry about snow or even very cold temperatures on the coast in the summer, but good rain gear is a must in every season. Though potable water is available at many sites along the way, backpackers should carry a water filter and/or purifying tablets in case they get caught short. It would be wise to carry at least two one-quart water bottles in case you need to stock up.

Hope for sun, and carry sunscreen. You'll want to wear light-weight, waterproof hiking boots with some ankle support, as the terrain is rough on some off-beach stretches of trail and they may help you get around rocky headlands without incident. Beach fires are nice, but backpackers should carry a lightweight stove for cooking. Mosquitoes are not a big problem in most places, but you might carry some repellent. A tide table is a must. Naturally you'll want a sleeping bag, pad, and tent.

Otherwise, the following list of Ten Essentials developed for day hikers by The Mountaineers should serve you well (though a topographical map and compass may amount to overkill on many of these hikes).

Extra clothing	First-aid kit
Extra food	Matches
Sunglasses	Flashlight
Knife	Map
Fire starter	Compass

Camping. Beach camping is permitted in Oregon, with two restrictions. No camping is allowed on the beach adjacent to a state park, and coastal towns often have municipal laws forbidding camping on the beach within city limits.

However, nearly all the seventeen Oregon state parks that are right along the beach have what are called hiker/biker camps—primitive tent sites that are usually some distance from motor home sites and whose fee ($2 in 1993) is a fraction of what car campers pay. For that you get a hot shower and access to plenty of clean drinking water, as well as a tent site. Hiker/biker sites are only for backpackers and cyclists, not car campers.

If you do camp on the beach, just be sure you're well above the high-tide line. There are also campsites along many of the forest trails that serve as coast trail links: Tillamook Head and Cape Falcon, for example. Access to potable water is the main limiting factor, but you may be able to stock up at a park and hike a few miles down to the beach to camp.

Drinking Water and Sanitation. State park campgrounds and waysides and Forest Service campgrounds are the most reliable sources of potable water for hikers. Water from coastal creeks, rivers, and lakes should be safe as long as you filter it or otherwise treat it to remove impurities.

Use developed toilet facilities whenever possible, since this is largely a civilized area—one well used by other people—that you're hiking through. Otherwise, be careful to bury wastes in dirt (not sand) a good distance from the trail or at least 200 feet from water sources. Don't burn toilet paper; pack it out.

Boating

Because this book focuses on nonmotorized recreation, references to boating are limited to suggestions for canoeing or sea kayaking. Kayaks are the craft of choice on open bays because their design generally allows them to maneuver well in wind and to resist swamping. Canoes may be preferable on small rivers or large creeks, though narrow lake fingers and bay sloughs may be quite suitable for canoeing as well. Maps indicate the location only of those boat launches mentioned in the text; there are many other boat landings along the coast in addition to these.

Cars on the Beach

Oregon's tradition of allowing cars on the beach isn't quite so distasteful if you remember that it's the tradition upon which the state legislature, later backed by the state Supreme Court, declared all of the state's beaches to be public up to the vegetation line (see Chapter 8). Over the years the state, at the urging of citizens, has slowly increased restrictions on beach driving. Now cars are allowed on only about 25 miles of beach; 14 of those miles are a continuous stretch between Fort Stevens State Park, just south of the Columbia River, and Gearhart (the "last bastion of beach driving in Oregon," as one state official characterizes it). In other places driving is permitted only from October through April, or only for pickups launching dory boats. Beach driving has been eliminated completely in Lincoln County.

Given these restrictions, cars aren't an issue on 90 percent of the state's beaches. Where cars are still allowed, think of the beach as a country road. Keep an eye peeled while you're walking, and don't set up your blanket and umbrella on the hard sand; stick to the higher, softer sand where drivers don't dare cruise.

A Final Word

Guidebooks aren't intended as a substitute for being there. This book gives specific, accurate, up-to-date information that will help you get where you want to go on the Oregon coast and offers just enough description to help you evaluate possible destinations. But there's plenty about the Oregon coast that can't be adequately described in a book: the groan of a 200-year-old Sitka spruce in a windstorm high up some cape, the feel of the sun on bare arms tucked into a hollow in the dunes, the clear sustained notes of a wrentit singing in the airy understory of an old-growth forest, the thrill of discovering a twenty-four-rayed sea star on the underside of a rock during a minus tide. There's a lot out there to discover. May this book be a catalyst for your own discoveries.

A Note About Safety

Safety is an important concern in all outdoor activities. No guidebook can alert you to every hazard or anticipate the limitations of every reader. Therefore, the descriptions of roads, trails, routes, and natural features in this book are not representations that a particular place or excursion will be safe for your party. When you follow any of the routes described in this book, you assume responsibility for your own safety. Under normal conditions, such excursions require the usual attention to traffic, road and trail conditions, weather, terrain, the capabilities of your party, and other factors. Keeping informed on current conditions and exercising common sense are the keys to a safe, enjoyable outing.

The Mountaineers

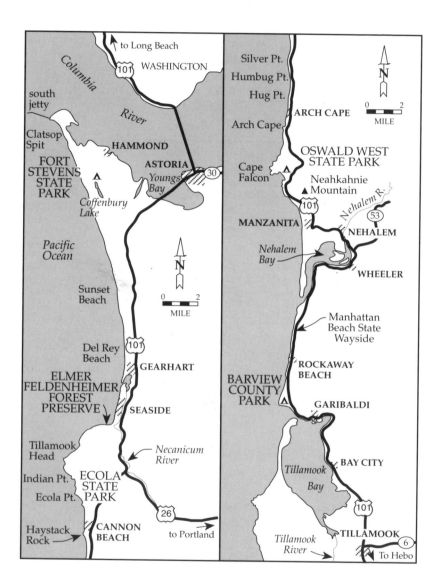

Opposite: *Footbridge spanning Short Sand Creek in Oswald West State Park*

The North Coast

Scrambling on the riprap at Columbia River's south jetty

1

Columbia River to Gearhart

Astoria is sometimes thought of as being the northernmost town on the Oregon coast, but in fact it's not on the coast at all; it's a good 10 miles inland. The first town a hiker walking south from the Columbia River's south jetty would reach is Gearhart, 15 miles south of the Columbia at the far end of the Clatsop Plains.

Fort Stevens State Park

From the jetty nearly to Warrenton, most of the beaches, dunes, lakes, and forest are part of Fort Stevens State Park, one of the state's most diverse and interesting parks. Birdwatchers are particularly drawn to the south jetty area, where a wide variety of birds (frequently including some unusual species) may be observed on the ocean beach, dunes, or estuary in the river's mouth. At Parking Area D, little trails lead down to the river, and a boardwalk leads to a concrete bird blind overlooking an estuary finger, where you may see nesting or wintering waterfowl. West of Parking Area C there's a tall wooden lookout you can climb to get a look at the river's mouth. The beach stretching to the south is also the official start of the nearly 400-mile Oregon Coast Trail.

About 4 miles south of the south jetty is what remains of the *Peter Iredale*, an English sailing ship that ran aground here in 1906. The rusting hulk that remains bears little resemblance to a ship at this point; still, it's rather remarkable that the salt and sea have left anything at all, nearly a century later.

South of the jetty and east of the beach, the park is divided into three main sections: a historic area to the north, a day-use area with additional historic sites in the middle, and the campground (reservations accepted in summer), the southern portion of which is adjacent to Coffenbury Lake.

History is a big part of the park's draw. Construction of Fort Stevens began during the Civil War; it was to be part of a "triangle of firepower" guarding the mouth of the Columbia. (The other two points of the triangle, Fort Canby and Fort Columbia, across the river in Washington, have also been converted to state parks.) A replica of the original earthwork fortification, along with six gun emplacements built just before World War I to guard the Columbia River, still remain. A World War I battery and a World War II gun emplacement are also open to the public.

Adjacent to the main batteries is a military museum and interpretive center with displays and artifacts tracing the fort's history. A 1954 Army cargo truck is used to take visitors on forty-five-minute narrated tours of the historical area in the summer. Guided tours of underground Battery Mishler are also offered in the summer.

With 9 miles of bicycle trails in the park, Fort Stevens is a great place to take your kids and bikes for some family cycling. Some bike routes parallel roads; most cut through the forest or across the dunes independent of auto routes.

On hot days, Coffenbury Lake is appealing for swimming, since it's out of the wind that blows on the beach most afternoons. There are two sandy swimming areas on the lake. Motorboats are allowed on the lake as well, but a speed limit of 10 miles per hour keeps wakes down and the atmosphere relatively tranquil. Most boaters on the lake are there to fish for perch, trout, crappie, and bass.

The park also has a number of designated hiking trails, but

Start of Oregon Coast Trail at south jetty, Fort Stevens State Park

Beaches and Sand

Where'd all that sand come from, anyway?

Basically from the mountains that back the beach, though in fact much of the Coast Range and foothills is built of sedimentary rock that itself began as sand 60 million years ago, when most of Oregon was under water. Eventually forces within the earth thrust that sea floor upward to create a mountain range. Rain and rivers began to erode that sandstone and other soft rock, carrying it out to sea and creating a huge reservoir of sand lying on the continental shelf.

Waves move the sand toward the shore, and prevailing winds blow it farther inland except where its movement is blocked by headlands, which are composed of harder volcanic rock. South of the Coquille River the beaches are primarily made of decomposed metamorphosed rock from the ancient Klamath Mountains; north of Tillamook Head, most of the sand came down the Columbia River.

It may look solid, but every beach is constantly moving: shifting north to south in summer and back north in winter, growing and shrinking with the seasons. Every winter the beach is cut back by high waves that push the sand into deeper waters, where it accumulates in offshore bars and creates two lines of breakers in winter. Come summer, low waves move the sand back on shore. The size of the sand grains on a particular beach determines the steepness of its slope: very fine sand creates the almost level Cannon Beach, for example, while the gravelly beach at the end of Yaquina Head has a relatively steep slope. Most beaches in Oregon are light tan in color, because most are composed mainly of quartz and feldspar grains. In some places, black-sand placer deposits create dark patches on the beach.

Though broken into pocket beaches by dozens of headlands, Oregon's nearly 400-mile coastline includes a total of 262 miles of sandy beach. The longest stretch of beach unbroken by rock is the 52 miles of beach running from Heceta Head to the mouth of Coos Bay, much of which is contained in the Oregon Dunes National Recreation Area.

most aren't really destination trails; they're primarily of interest to families camping at the park who might want to do some exploring on foot. Some of the hiking trails are dirt paths; others are paved with asphalt and are parallel to bike routes. Circumnavigation of Coffenbury Lake makes a nice outing, especially early on a summer morning, when you're likely to see water birds or hear songbirds in the brushy forest.

To reach Fort Stevens State Park, follow signs from US 101 just south of the Youngs Bay Bridge at Astoria. As you head north on Ridge Road, the first park entrance you'll encounter is the campground entrance; take it to reach Coffenbury Lake or the beach by the shipwreck. The road to the day-use areas and the south jetty is 0.5 mile north of the campground entrance. Continuing north on Ridge Road, the entrance to the historic area is at the edge of the town of Hammond.

Coffenbury Lake Trail

2.2-mile loop

Follow the park's campground road past the entrance station and turn left into the parking area at Coffenbury Lake. For a counter-clockwise hike from the picnic area at the lake's north end, pick up the trail along the shoreline near the restrooms. It follows the lake's edge and then ventures into the woods for a distance. At the far end the trail meets an old road; take it across the lake's marshy south end and veer left where the footpath resumes. Walk through the picnic and swimming area on the lake's east side and drop back into the northeastern corner of the parking lot to return to your starting point.

The ocean beach stretches south uninterrupted to the mouth of the Necanicum River at Gearhart. In addition to access at the south jetty and the *Peter Iredale* in Fort Stevens State Park, and at Gearhart, there are access roads at Sunset Beach and Del Rey Beach. Controversial as they have been, however, cars are allowed on the beach along the Clatsop Plains—something to be aware of if you're planning to walk along this stretch of beach. North of the *Peter Iredale* they're prohibited on summer afternoons (May 1 to September 15, noon to midnight); from the *Peter Iredale* south to Gearhart driving is unrestricted, though the maximum allowable speed is 25 miles per hour. Keep an eye out for cars, and/or walk on the softer dry sand for safety's sake.

2

Seaside to Hug Point

From Gearhart, the wide beach stretches south to Arch Cape, interrupted only by massive Tillamook Head. The vastness of these
northern beaches, and their proximity to Portland, make them
popular year-round. Seaside Beach is a particularly busy place in
summer; you can take a civilized stroll along the "prom" or get
brave and take a dip in the ocean (lifeguards are on duty in summer). South of Tillamook Head, you find more solitude the farther
south you go from Cannon Beach, though homes line the bluffs all
the way to Arch Cape. The beach is so wide here that it never really
feels crowded, except during the Sand Castle Contest in June—then
it's positively claustrophobic for a half-mile or so. Long-distance
beach walkers can go from Cannon Beach clear to Arch Cape if they
time their walk right; Silver, Hug, and Humbug points can all be
rounded at low tide in summer. Hug Point is a particularly interesting

Looking south to Ecola Point from Indian Beach

spot; from the day-use area off US 101, walk north to investigate the point's wave-sculpted cliffs and caves.

In Seaside, Necanicum Estuary Park may offer decent bird watching in the right conditions; it's directly across North Holladay Drive from Seaside High School and serves as a laboratory for marine science students at the school. Stairs lead down to the mud flats from the road.

Haystack Rock, on Cannon Beach, is not only one of the most photographed landmarks on the coast but one of its biological gems as well. The exquisite tidepools at its base are among a handful of state-designated "marine gardens," where no collecting of any marine invertebrates is allowed. The rock itself is protected as part of the Oregon Islands National Wildlife Refuge. It's a major nesting site for western gulls, pelagic cormorants, pigeon guillemots, and tufted puffins—in fact, it hosts one of the largest and most easily watched colonies of nesting puffins on the Oregon coast. A naturalist is frequently on hand here in summer, especially at low tide, when touch tanks may be set up to satisfy those who aren't content with just looking.

Ecola State Park

Ecola State Park and Elmer Feldenheimer Forest Preserve comprise a large, contiguous tract of forest land draping Tillamook Head; both are managed by state parks. For hikers, the trail over Tillamook Head is the centerpiece of this stretch of coastline. It follows essentially the same route Captain William Clark and his party took to what is now known as Cannon Beach during the Lewis and Clark expedition's overwintering at Fort Clatsop in 1805–06. Their journal reports that they walked from the fort to the mouth of Ecola Creek one day to investigate reports of a beached whale.

There are several ways to approach a hike here, depending upon how long you want to hike and whether a one-way hike is an option. With a shuttle car, you can make a one-way trek over the headland from Seaside south to Indian Beach or Ecola Point. A southward hike is preferable; you get most of the elevation gain out of the way in the first 1.5 miles, after which it's an enjoyable rolling or gently descending trek. For a loop hike out of Indian Beach, take the main trail north 2.3 miles to Clark's Viewpoint, then backtrack to the trail junction near the outhouses, and return via the old road above Indian Creek. This southernmost trail section can be

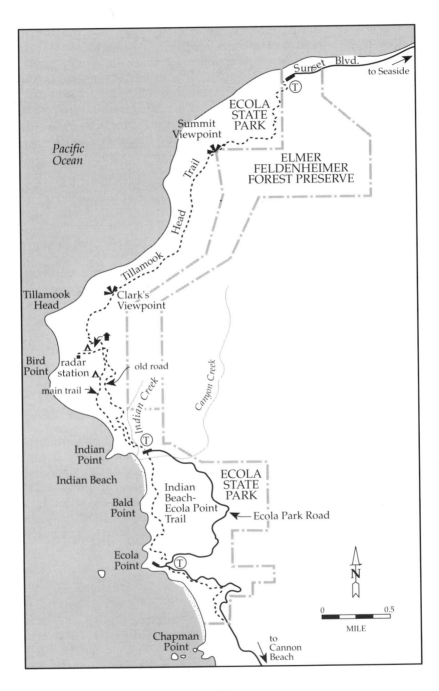

unbelievably muddy, even in summertime, making the Indian Creek road a good alternative. Mountain bikes aren't allowed on the park's footpaths, but they are allowed on the old roads. There's interesting tidepooling at both Ecola Point and Indian Beach. At either beach, follow the trail down to the beach and head south 0.25 to 0.5 mile until you reach the rocky intertidal area. With a shuttle car you can enjoy a one-way hike between Ecola Point and Indian Beach on a link in the Oregon Coast Trail that follows the bluff above the shore.

Tillamook Head Trail

6 miles, 900-foot elevation gain

From US 101 in Seaside, turn west at the traffic light at Avenue U. Drive 0.2 mile, turn left onto South Edgewood Road, and follow the road 1.2 miles (it becomes Sunset Boulevard) until it ends at a trailhead parking area. Follow trail signs onto the main trail. (At about 0.25 mile another trail comes in from the right; continue straight, bearing right shortly at another unmarked junction.)

After about 0.5 mile the trail steepens and begins switchbacking up the hillside. At 1.5 miles a spur leads to a gravel clearing at the summit of the headland—trees block the view west, but you can gaze east toward the Coast Range—and then loops back to the main trail. From here the trail rolls along the headland, offering occasional ocean views, including one at Clark's Viewpoint (3.7 miles), where Captain William Clark reportedly stopped to take in the view nearly 200 years ago.

Continuing, the trail slowly descends, switchbacking briefly just before reaching a campsite, primitive outhouse, and a trail junction at 4.4 miles. A short walk west leads to the site of an old radar station from World War II. The main trail continues south down the head to Indian Beach. Alternately, head east at the trail junction here, following the sign to Indian Creek; shortly the old road it follows veers south and winds up back at the Indian Beach parking area.

Indian Beach–Ecola Point Trail

1.5 miles

From Cannon Beach, follow signs to Ecola State Park. For a north-south hike, drive to the end of the road at Indian Beach and pick up the trail toward the beach. After crossing a creek, veer left at the junction and take up the trail toward Ecola Point. It rolls

Oregon Coast Trail hikers southbound over Tillamook Head

along 100 feet or more above the ocean, in and out of the woods, offering good views of the remote shoreline. The trail breaks out of the forest at the edge of the Ecola Point parking area.

Another footpath, a link in the Oregon Coast Trail, begins just south of the Ecola Point parking area along the main road, but it follows a route parallel and fairly close to the road, and is mainly of interest to those traveling by foot toward Cannon Beach rather than day hikers looking for an off-road outing.

Headlands, Sea Stacks, Arches, and Blowholes

About two-thirds of the Oregon shoreline consists of beaches; the other third is rocky headlands that stalwartly resist the pounding of countless waves. They and the many sea stacks standing just offshore exist because they're made of tough volcanic rock, rather than the sandstone, mudstone, and siltstone that have already been eroded, or are in the process thereof, elsewhere on the coast. Many of the coast's tidepools are formed of basalt bedrock, some easily recognizable as lava.

For example, Tillamook Head, Hug Point, Arch Cape, and Cape Falcon on the north coast were formed by basalt flows sandwiched between layers of mudstone or sandstone. Neahkahnie Mountain, Cape Lookout, and Yaquina Head are examples of the Miocene-epoch volcanoes that probably began as offshore islands some 20 million years ago. Cape Perpetua is formed of lava that flowed out of undersea vents some 40 million years ago, hardening into a massive chunk of basalt that eventually uplifted to form the towering headland. Many of the capes and sea stacks of the south coast are of older origin than even the volcanic rock in the north. Humbug Mountain on the south coast is composed of gravelly conglomerate deposited more than 100 million years ago. And Cape Kiwanda is a sandstone headland, sculpted but not yet destroyed by waves thanks to the protection of a basalt sea stack just offshore.

The same process that creates headlands and sea stacks—natural erosion of rocks of varying composition—is responsible for the many blowholes, spouting horns, cauldrons, and natural arches found along the coast. Some result from a particular pattern of erosion in a sandstone slab, such as the blowhole at Smelt Sands Wayside north of Yachats. Others, such as Devil's Churn at Cape Perpetua, create a show when waves smash into an enlarged crack in ancient basalt. Devil's Punchbowl, north of Newport, was formed when the roofs collapsed on sea caves formed of sandstone.

3

Arch Cape to Manzanita

This section of the Oregon coast claims the longest stretch of Oregon Coast Trail unbroken by road crossings—6.5 miles. There are only two highway crossings in the 13 contiguous miles of trail from Arch Cape to the south side of Neahkahnie Mountain. That's nice for long-distance hikers—and it's great for day hikers because of the varied hiking opportunities it presents.

Dominating this section of coastline is Oswald West State Park, a large, forested park incorporating Cape Falcon and Neahkahnie Mountain, two major north coast landmarks. A series of three parking areas, signed Oswald West State Park, are clustered near the confluence of Short Sand and Necarney creeks; though Neahkahnie Mountain is actually within the park's boundaries, it has its own trailhead parking areas and is discussed separately.

Oswald West State Park

Within Oswald West State Park there are several opportunities for hikers—and campers, surfers, and tidepoolers. Short Sand Beach is popular among surfers year-round. At low tide, explore the pools at either the north or south ends of the crescent beach.

The campground here is unique among state parks on the coast; it's a pack-in site, complete with wheelbarrows to help campers transport their gear 0.3 mile from highway to tent site. Use the southernmost of the three parking areas to reach the campground, the middle parking lot for beach access, and the northernmost lot to begin hikes northward toward Cape Falcon (though link trails connect all the trails at one point or another).

Hikers have all kinds of options here. A popular day hike is the 2.5-mile walk out to the tip of Cape Falcon. Along the way you cross trickling creeks, listen to forest songbirds, and grab occasional southward views. Cape Falcon is a fair vantage point from which to spot whales. Carry binoculars not only to watch for whales but to watch the surfers far below off Short Sand Beach.

For a short hike into some magnificent old-growth forest, stroll south a little ways on the Oregon Coast Trail from where it

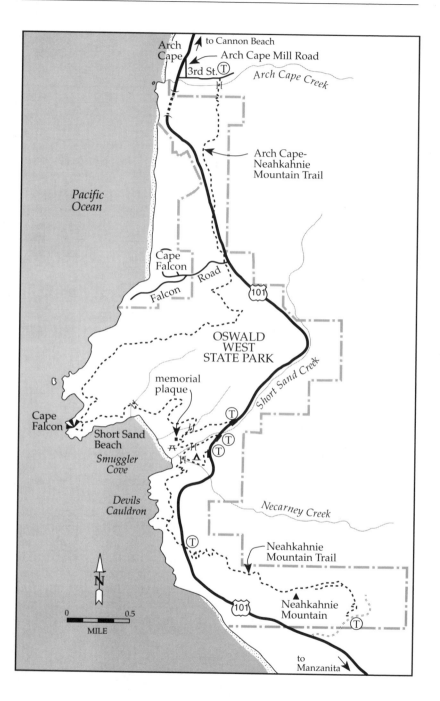

Nehalem valley and bay from Neahkahnie Mountain

resumes in the community of Arch Cape. For families with young children, a walk from any of the Oswald West State Park parking areas to the beach, along interconnecting trails, and over footbridges, with time at the beach to splash and dig, makes a satisfying day's outing.

Arch Cape to Neahkahnie Mountain Trail
8.5 miles, 1,200-foot elevation gain

The longest unbroken forested stretch of the Oregon Coast Trail begins in the community of Arch Cape. A short distance north of the US 101 highway tunnel, turn east onto Arch Cape Mill Road, turning left with the road in a short distance. The trail, marked by a post, starts at the south end of Third Street. (If you're leaving a car here, note that it's a residential neighborhood, so choose your parking spot thoughtfully.) The trail begins with a suspension footbridge over Arch Cape Creek next to its confluence with a cascading side stream. Follow the trail up about 0.1 mile, turning right at the trail post pointing toward Cape Falcon.

Here the trail carries hikers around the back side of Arch Cape, climbing gradually through a lovely climax forest. At about 1 mile the sight and sound of the ocean return; shortly the trail turns onto an old road and begins a descent toward US 101, hitting the highway at about 1.75 miles. Walk south about 50 yards and pick up the trail across the road.

The next mile or so stays within earshot, and sometimes sight, of US 101, rolling along through lovely old-growth forest and crossing the road into the community of Cape Falcon at about 2.5 miles. The trail eventually veers west, leaving the highway noise behind. It rolls along for a while and then begins an ascent, steep in places, to an old blow-down area that was logged over some years ago. As the trail starts to crest the ridge (at about 3.5 miles), look back toward the north for a glimpse up the coast and of Haystack Rock.

The trail now drops steadily until it reaches the sea cliff and begins rolling along the shoreline, offering occasional views. At 4.5 miles, a clear—but unmarked—spur trail leads out through waist-high salal onto the cape's treeless tip; there, a maze of trails cuts through the brush leading to various viewpoints north and south.

Continuing south, the trail rolls along, following the contours of the hillside. At about 5.2 miles it enters a clearing, offering good views south to Neahkahnie Mountain and Short Sand Beach. At 7 miles a trail junction offers the option of heading east 0.5 mile to the northernmost parking area for Oswald West State Park (about 10 miles south of Cannon Beach; begin here for a round-trip day hike out to Cape Falcon). Otherwise bear right, following the sign about 0.25 mile to the picnic area overlooking the beach.

The trail resumes at the southeast corner of the picnic area. The route through the park is a little confusing due to a proliferation of trails, but signs (and the map accompanying this trail description) should help. Cross a bridge over Short Sand Creek, bear right at the next junction, continue west a short distance, cross a suspension bridge over Necarney Creek, and begin switchbacking fairly steeply up the hillside. About 0.5 mile from Necarney Creek the grade moderates, heading south not far from US 101. Pass through a tunnel of vegetation and emerge onto a grassy hillside. Shortly you'll pass a spur trail (it leads west 0.1 mile to a fenced overlook above the churning sea)

Skunk cabbage

Skunk Cabbage

Ever noticed how sweet the fragrance of skunk cabbage blossoms are? Probably not; the blossoms' perfume tends to get lost in the decidedly rank odor emanating from the plant's stem and massive leaves.

As skunklike as its smell may be, *Lysichitum americanum* is one of the most reliable harbingers of spring on the Oregon coast, brightening shady forest bogs as early as February with bright yellow spathes hooding a pokerlike flower stem covered with hundreds of tiny, greenish flowers, and large leaves measuring two, three, even four or five feet long. Perhaps it's an acquired affinity, but even the odor can be welcome after a long winter.

This tropical-looking Northwest plant is related to the taro root eaten in the South Pacific. Like taro, skunk cabbage root was reportedly roasted and pounded into flour by coastal natives (cooking neutralizes the toxic calcium oxalate contained in the plant). Various tribes also made medicines from the roots and leaves to ease childbirth, soothe cuts, and salve ringworm, among other uses. Bears and elk are fond of the roots, sometimes digging up whole bogs.

The following Kathlamet Indian story, from Leslie L. Haskin's *Wild Flowers of the Pacific Coast*, relates some of the significance skunk cabbage had for coastal tribes:

In the ancient days, they say, there was no salmon. The Indians had nothing to eat save roots and leaves. Principally among these was the skunk cabbage. Finally the spring salmon came for the first time. As they passed up the river, a person stood upon the shore and shouted: "Here come our relatives whose bodies are full of eggs! If it had not been for me all the people would have starved."

"Who speaks to us?" asked the salmon.

"Your uncle, Skunk Cabbage," was the reply.

Then the salmon went ashore to see him, and as a reward for having fed the people he was given an elk-skin blanket and a war club, and was set in the rich, soft soil near the river. There he stands to this day, wrapped in his elk-skin blanket and holding aloft his war club.

before the trail heads up to meet US 101 at a trailhead shared with Neahkahnie Mountain.

Neahkahnie Mountain

Neahkahnie Mountain was a vision-quest site for the original residents of this coastline, and still is—in a less formal sense—for many contemporary hikers. While some seek inner visions, others are content just with the magnificent views southward from Neahkahnie to the Nehalem River Valley. In spring look for white trillium, pink salmonberry, and other wildflowers along the trail; we heard the whump-whump sound of a grouse on our last ascent. It's lovely to hike up the south side and down the north side, which is longer and winds back into beautiful old-growth forest, if you have a shuttle car or if you don't mind hiking a couple of miles along US 101 and up a gravel road to complete the loop.

Neahkahnie Mountain Trail

4.5 miles (1.5 miles from south trailhead to summit, 890-foot elevation gain; 3 miles from north trailhead to summit, 1,200-foot elevation gain)

To reach the south trailhead, turn east off US 101 about 1.5 miles north of Manzanita (or 13 miles south of Cannon Beach) at the hiker sign and drive 0.5 mile up a bumpy gravel road to a trailhead parking area. From the Oregon Coast Trail (OCT) marker post, the trail climbs steadily, varying between dark stands of Sitka spruce and open, brushy slopes with outstanding views. At 1.2 miles there's an OCT post on the summit ridge. To reach the summit, bear left up an old road toward a collection of telecommunications antennas; a rough trail continues around the building to the knobby summit.

To continue down the north side, return to the ridgetop junction and pick up the trail leading south at a slow ascent around the back side of the mountain. About 0.5 mile beyond the junction the trail reaches the southern ridge, enters a clearing, and then begins dropping down through magnificent old-growth forest, first with shorter switchbacks and later with long traverses. Minutes from the bottom it emerges from the woods and leads across the open hillside to end on US 101 about 1.5 miles north of where the southern trailhead access road leaves the highway, and across the highway from where the Oregon Coast Trail continues to the south toward Cape Falcon.

4

Nehalem to Tillamook

The beaches between *Neahkahnie Mountain* and the mouth of Tillamook Bay are long and accessible, broken only by the Nehalem River emptying into the sea. Parts of each beach stretch are often busy with kite flyers and other beachgoers, such as at the towns of Manzanita and Rockaway Beach. But walk long enough and you can reach lonelier stretches, such as Nehalem Spit or the mile or so of beach north of Barview County Park at the mouth of Tillamook Bay.

A particularly interesting beach walk would be one starting at the day-use area at Nehalem Bay State Park (see park description below) and ending at Manhattan Beach Wayside or another point to the south. The challenge—and the fun—of the trip is crossing the mouth of Nehalem Bay. Jetty Fishery, along US 101 at the mouth of Nehalem Bay, regularly shuttles beach hikers across the bay. Often they're long-distance trekkers, but day hikers use the shuttle as

Windsurfer on Nehalem Bay

well. For more information on the boat shuttle, see Section 4 of the Oregon Coast Trail chapter. If you don't have a second car for a shuttle back to your starting point, consider a simple round-trip walk from the park's day-use area to the end of Nehalem Spit and back. The unobstructed beach offers unlimited walking for 7 miles between Nehalem and Tillamook bays; much of the way there are homes near or along the shore, though they fall away as you approach Barview County Park, at Tillamook Bay's north jetty. The county park offers rather spartan camping facilities but dramatic views where the huge bay—fed by five rivers—meets the Pacific; it's a good spot for winter storm watching.

Kayaking. Tillamook Bay is an interesting, and sometimes challenging, place to spend a day sea kayaking. The bird watching changes with the seasons, and from a boat in midbay, you get a fresh perspective on the coastal landscape. It's huge, but shallow in many places, enough so that kayakers can easily get stranded on mud flats at low tide. The best put-in is at Memaloose boat launch at the south end of the bay, off Bayocean Road. From here, particularly if the wind is high or the tide is low, you can paddle southeast into the salt marsh where the Trask and Tillamook rivers enter the bay. Otherwise, you could ride an outgoing tide out into the bay (to avoid getting stranded, veer right along the inside of a line of pilings reaching toward the center of the bay before heading north) and follow the incoming tide back to the boat launch.

Nehalem Bay is also appealing for exploring by kayak. There are boat ramps in the towns of Nehalem and Wheeler, but the most versatile put-in is at the ramp just south of the US 101 bridge over the Nehalem River; from here you can paddle upstream into the river if it's a windy day, or downstream into the salt marsh and open bay if it's calm.

Nehalem Bay State Park

Nehalem Bay State Park occupies the north spit at the mouth of the bay. In addition to a 291-site campground, the park has a horse camp and 7.5 miles of equestrian trail, plus 1.5 miles of bike trail. It also has the unique distinction of being accessible by air; the 2,400-foot landing strip at Nehalem Airport is 0.25 mile from the campground entrance, between the park and the bay. Use the park as a jumping-off point to explore the beach, walking south onto Nehalem Spit or north to Manzanita at the base of Neahkahnie Mountain.

Bald Eagles

Stand alongside any bay on the Oregon coast and eventually you'll see a bald eagle. Every major estuary on the coast has at least one nesting pair of the huge birds, and those that nest here winter here as well. Winter is a good time to spot bald eagles on the coast, because in addition to the year-round residents, a number of birds migrate in from Alaska, Montana, and Canada to winter here, too.

Bald eagles feed primarily on fish and waterfowl. As a result, they're never far from water. They nest high in very large trees, building huge nests (7 to 8 feet across) on a foundation of sticks and softening them with a lining of moss, grass, feathers, and pine needles. When they're not soaring high over a bay or above the open ocean, bald eagles may be seen perched on tall snags above the water. When you're out on a high headland looking for whales, keep an eye peeled for a large bird with a bright white head soaring along the cliffs.

Bald eagle

The bald eagle's reproductive success has not been as good on the Oregon coast as in other parts of the state, but they are holding their own here and even slowly increasing in number. Wildlife officials aren't yet certain why the coastal eagles aren't reproducing well, but they suspect that agricultural and industrial contaminants (such as dioxins, DDTs, and PCBs) from the Columbia River may be a factor. Human disturbance near nests is another factor adversely affecting bald eagle nesting success on the coast. Wildlife officials urge visitors to obey all trail-closure signs and to use only marked trails, particularly in or near refuges.

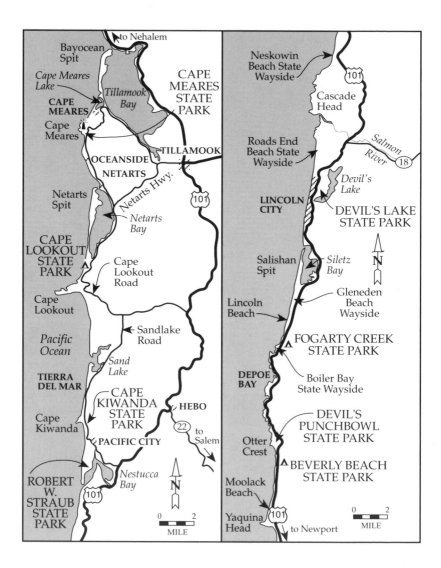

Bayocean
Spit

to Nehalem

CAPE
MEARES
STATE
PARK

Cape Meares
Lake

Tillamook
Bay

**CAPE
MEARES**

Cape
Meares

TILLAMOOK

OCEANSIDE

NETARTS

Netarts Hwy.

Netarts
Spit

101

Netarts
Bay

**CAPE
LOOKOUT
STATE
PARK**

Cape
Lookout
Road

Cape
Lookout

Sandlake
Road

Pacific
Ocean

Sand
Lake

**TIERRA
DEL MAR**

**CAPE
KIWANDA
STATE
PARK**

HEBO

Cape
Kiwanda

22

to
Salem

PACIFIC CITY

**ROBERT
W.
STRAUB
STATE
PARK**

Nestucca
Bay

101

N

0   2
MILE

Neskowin
Beach State
Wayside

101

Cascade
Head

Roads End
Beach State
Wayside

Salmon
River
18

Devil's
Lake

**LINCOLN
CITY**

**DEVIL'S LAKE
STATE PARK**

Salishan
Spit

Siletz
Bay

N

Gleneden
Beach
Wayside

Lincoln
Beach

**FOGARTY CREEK
STATE PARK**

**DEPOE
BAY**

Boiler Bay
State Wayside

**DEVIL'S
PUNCHBOWL
STATE PARK**

Otter
Crest

**BEVERLY BEACH
STATE PARK**

Moolack
Beach

Yaquina
Head

101

to Newport

0   2
MILE

Opposite: *Beach at Lincoln City*

The North-Central Coast

5

Bayocean Spit to Cape Lookout

To see what's known as the Three Capes area, leave US 101 at Tillamook (or Pacific City, northbound); it's well worth the detour. Each of the three capes has its own personality and appeal: Cape Meares is topped by a historic lighthouse and surrounded by a federal wildlife refuge; the tip of fingerlike Cape Lookout is a good bet for spotting whales during the winter or spring migration; and sandstone Cape Kiwanda (see Chapter 6) offers the best sand-dune sliding on the north coast. Camping is available at Cape Lookout State Park and at several private RV parks.

From the town of Oceanside you can see Three Arch Rocks, the site of Oregon's largest seabird colonies and the state's first

Northbound on Bayocean Spit Trail

coastal bird refuge. You'll need binoculars to get a good view. There's also a small tidepool area at the base of Maxwell Point, just east of Three Arch Rocks; park in the Oceanside Beach Wayside at the north end of town. For an unusual beach day hike, prearrange a boat shuttle across the mouth of the bay at Netarts and down Netarts Spit to the campground at Cape Lookout.

Kayaking. Netarts Bay makes for excellent kayaking; you'll nearly always see seals and plenty of waterfowl. It's best to launch during an incoming tide, as the put-in at Netarts is very close to the mouth of the bay and can quickly pull inexperienced boaters into a dangerous situation if the tide is running out and the wind is blowing offshore.

Bayocean Spit

In 1906 a real estate broker from Kansas City envisioned a second Atlantic City on the sand spit separating Tillamook Bay from the Pacific Ocean. By 1914 as many as 600 building lots had been sold in what was called Bay Ocean Park, and it was becoming a bustling community. But the unstable spit couldn't support the development. Lots began eroding steadily, and in 1950 the last house on the spit washed into the sea.

Now Bayocean Spit is better known as one of the hottest bird watching spots in the state, especially during the fall shorebird migration from early August through early October. Then you'll find lots of action on the mud flats (especially right after high tide), but there's plenty of birding action in the forest, the dunes, and around Cape Meares Lake as well. The bay is full of waterfowl in the winter, and orcas are sometimes seen in the bay as well.

The Bayocean Spit Trail is popular among hikers, but it also attracts mountain bikers. The route follows an old roadbed, making for easy cycling. There are a couple of campsites (protected from the wind by groves of trees) near the end of the trail for relatively remote overnight camping.

To get to Bayocean Spit from US 101 in Tillamook, follow signs to Three Capes Scenic Route west and north about 8 miles. Watch for the big sign describing the spit's history on the bay side of the road. Turn off the main highway and drive north 1 mile on graveled Bayocean Dike Road. Park at the road's end. The main trail to the tip of the spit leads north out of the parking area; there's also a 0.3-mile trail to the beach that leads through the dunes from the northwest corner of the parking area.

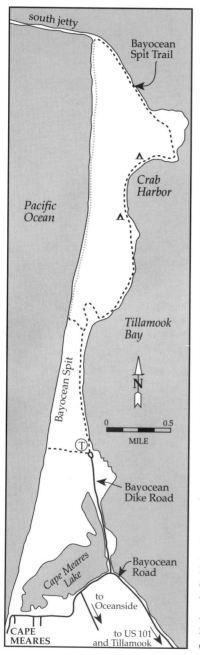

Bayocean Spit Trail
4 miles (beach-trail loop, 7.3 miles)

The trailhead is at the end of Bayocean Dike Road (see driving directions above). From the parking area at the end of the road, the trail leads straight north, following the bay shore and offering expansive bay views. At about 1 mile the trail splits, with a left turn leading 0.2 mile on a sandy trail over the foredune and down onto the beach. Bearing right, the trail passes a gate and enters the forest. At about 1.4 miles it rises slightly, curves, and then drops back down to the bay shore. Near 2.5 miles a cozy campsite appears in the trees off the trail to the left, and there's another campsite a short distance farther, near a rock with a plaque commemorating completion of Tillamook Bay's south jetty in 1979. A couple of minutes farther down the trail there's a two-seater outhouse in a meadow off to the right. The last 0.6 mile of trail is along the windy tip of the spit, ending at the south jetty.

If you're mountain biking, return as you came. Hikers have the option of making a loop by following the beach south about 2.3 miles to where the pine-topped dune to the left drops to merge with the grass-covered foredune. About 25 yards from the end of the forested hill, look for a trail (barely discernible) leading up and over

48

the foredune to meet the main trail and follow it south about 1 mile back to where you started.

Cape Meares State Park

The focal point, so to speak, of Cape Meares State Park is the 1890 lighthouse atop the cape. It's no longer in service; instead, an automated beacon activated in 1963 shines from a concrete block house just behind the old lighthouse. But the old one is currently the only lighthouse in Oregon that visitors can enter and get a close-up view of its huge crystal Fresnel lens, which was hand-ground in France in 1887. The lighthouse is open daily in summer and on weekends in spring and fall.

Surrounding the state park is Cape Meares National Wildlife Refuge, established in 1938 to protect seabird nesting habitat. Most of the refuge is covered with old-growth Sitka spruce and western hemlock, but its vertical sea cliffs are where tufted puffins, pelagic cormorants, and pigeon guillemots nest. More recently the refuge has been recognized as an important nesting site for bald eagles as well. Looking west from the lighthouse, especially in the morning, you may catch a glimpse of an eagle hunting above the offshore islands; puffins are most likely to be seen from the south side of the walk down to the lighthouse. The largest rock off the tip of the cape has a very large colony of common murres. A portion of the Oregon Coast Trail used to lead through the refuge, but it's now closed, due both to landslides and the need to protect nesting birds from disturbance by humans.

Cape Meares may actually be best known for an oddity called the Octopus Tree. The tree is a short walk from the lighthouse parking area, and it's quite

Cape Meares lighthouse

49

impressive: a massive Sitka spruce with six arms instead of a central trunk. While you're in the neighborhood, take a short walk to check out another impressive Sitka spruce, called the Big Spruce, notable not for any contortions but for its size.

From the top of Cape Meares you can walk down to the beach—nice if you're in the mood for some aerobic exercise on the walk back up, or if you have a shuttle car to pick you up at the oceanside community of Cape Meares, about 0.7 mile by beach (or 0.9 mile by trail) to the east. Or make a loop hike by taking the high-tide trail into town and then walking back on the beach to pick up the trail again (3.4 miles total).

To reach Cape Meares State Park from US 101 in Tillamook, follow signs west and northwest to Three Capes Scenic Route about 10 miles, past the community of Cape Meares, to the park at the top of the headland.

Octopus Tree Trail
0.75 mile

The trail begins at the end of 1-mile Lighthouse Road leading into the park. Pick up the trail heading south past the restrooms. Walk a couple of minutes to the Octopus Tree, which is enclosed by a wooden fence, presumably to discourage climbing. Continuing on the trail, pass a stellar view southward of Three Arch Rocks and Maxwell Point. The trail gently descends to cross a creek and then gradually ascends to end at the highway about 0.6 mile south of the park entrance road.

Big Spruce Trail
0.2 mile

The trailhead is hard to spot from a moving car; it's just inside the woods on the north side of the entrance to Cape Meares State Park. Bear left, following the sign, to where the trail ends by circling the huge tree.

Cape Meares Beach Trail
1 mile, 500-foot elevation gain

The trail shares a trailhead with the Big Spruce Trail. Bear right, following the sign, down through the Sitka spruce forest. Shortly the trail wanders out of the old growth and into a logged area now dominated by alders. The grade is moderate to steep down to a junction at 0.8 mile; to reach the beach, continue straight

0.2 mile. A right turn puts you on the High Tide Trail into Cape Meares.

High Tide Trail
0.9 mile, 200-foot elevation gain

This trail is an alternative pedestrian route, between the bottom of the Cape Meares Beach Trail and the community of Cape Meares. Its south trailhead is at the south end of Fifth Street in Cape Meares; a gate blocks the road, but hikers may continue up the old roadbed, now a link in the Oregon Coast Trail. The trail climbs gently through the alder forest, eventually becoming a narrow footpath and gaining about 100 feet, before beginning a slow descent to a small creek near the base of Cape Meares. The trail crosses the creek, heads up a short distance, and meets the Cape Meares Beach Trail.

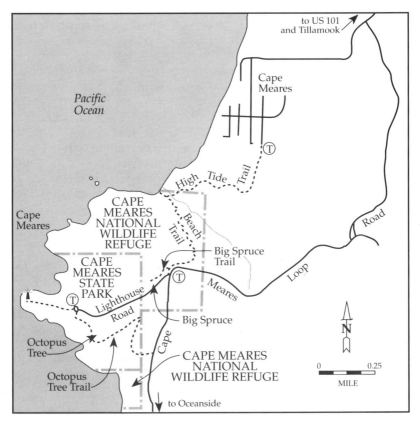

Cape Lookout State Park

Cape Lookout, a steep-cliffed promontory extending nearly 2 miles due west into the Pacific, is a wonderful destination for hikers. Options range from a 10-mile round trip from the campground to the tip of the cape to a 0.25-mile loop hike with children on the Cape Lookout Nature Trail, adjacent to the campground. (Pick up a trail guide brochure, with descriptions corresponding to sixteen marked stations, at the campground registration booth.) In between, consider a beach walk to the end of Netarts Spit, a hike from the summit of the cape down to a rather secluded beach on the cape's south side, and an out-and-back walk to the tip of the cape.

The last-mentioned hike is probably the most popular, especially in mid-March (and in late December through early January, if the weather's decent). The reason: the 400-foot-high promontory is considered one of the best sites for whale watching on the Oregon coast, especially during the spring and winter migrations. You may even see a whale in summer, since more than 200 gray whales are known to spend summers off the Oregon coast now. Whales may pass as close as 100 yards, but binoculars always improve wildlife viewing. Be prepared for mud on the trail in rainy periods.

There's a bouldery tidepool area near the base of the cape at the bottom of the cape beach hike.

To reach Cape Lookout State Park from US 101 in Tillamook, follow signs west toward Three Capes Scenic Route. After crossing the Tillamook River, either turn north to loop around Cape Meares or turn south to cut directly west toward Netarts and south to Cape Lookout. The state park campground (which accepts reservations in summer) is about 10 miles from US 101 via the Netarts Highway.

Cape Lookout Trail
2.5 miles, 400-foot elevation change

The trail begins at a trailhead parking area off Cape Lookout Road, 2.8 miles south of the entrance to Cape Lookout State Park campground. Two trails start side by side. The trail on the right leads toward the campground (see below). To hike out to the tip of the cape, take the left-hand trail, continuing due west at the junction with the beach trail (see below). The trail rolls west, gradually descending, passing a southward viewpoint at 0.6 mile and a northward viewpoint at 1.2 miles. The route returns to the south side of the cliffs, offering occasional views; listen for the moan of the offshore buoy as you approach the trail's end at the cape's tip.

Cape Lookout Beach Trail
2 miles, 840-foot elevation loss

Begin on the trail to Cape Lookout's tip (see above), but make a sharp left turn down the hill at the trail junction some 75 yards from the trailhead. From here the trail descends gently through an old-growth Sitka spruce forest, crossing a creek at about the half-way point and switchbacking now and then. The trail ends close to the base of the cape. If you have a shuttle car to pick you up, continue south down the beach about 4 miles to the ORV area at the end of Galloway Road. The first mile or so from the end of the beach trail is off limits to ORVs, but you may encounter them on the rest of your walk.

Cape Lookout Campground Trail
2.5 miles, 840-foot elevation loss

Beginning at the Cape Lookout trailhead parking area (see

Waist-high in beach grass on Netarts Spit

above), take the right-hand trail leading out from the west end of the parking area. It follows a rolling grade north through the woods, crossing Cape Creek at about 0.9 mile. At 1.3 miles a spur trail leads a short distance to Cape Lookout Road; continue north, following the trail as it descends through the woods toward the park's picnic area, just south of the campground. Near the end, the trail joins a gravel service road. In the day-use area, spur trails give you various options; pick one and continue north to the campground or veer west onto the beach. The nature trail is off the main trail leading toward the campground.

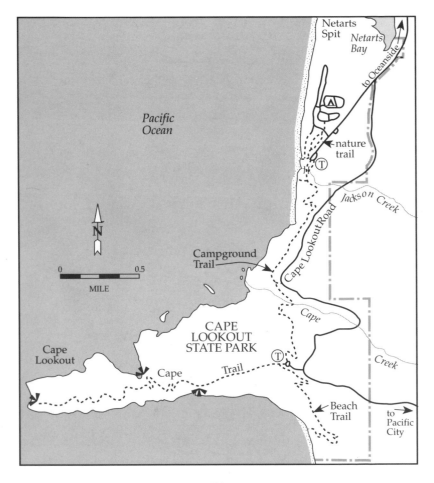

Tip of Cape Lookout from Cape Lookout Beach Trail

On US 101

If you're bypassing Three Capes Scenic Route, traveling on US 101 instead, consider a walk and a picnic at Munson Creek Falls, something of a surprise along this route.

Munson Creek Falls Trail

0.25 mile

Look for a sign on the highway 7 miles south of Tillamook and follow the road 1.5 miles east to the gravel parking area. The trail to the right leads to a picnic spot at the base of the 266-foot waterfall. A precipitous upper trail (0.3 mile) used to lead along a cliff-hugging path and wooden walkways to a higher viewpoint, but it's been closed since a massive mudslide took out a chunk of the trail. It's still possible to negotiate the route, but do so at your own risk. Park personnel don't expect to reconstruct the trail anytime in the near future.

Tufted Puffins

Early Oregonians called them sea parrots because of their bright red, triangle-shaped beaks. But it's their breeding plumage—white facial feathers with straw-colored plumes curving back behind the eyes, contrasting starkly with a glossy black body—that makes tufted puffins such recognizable summer nesters on Oregon's offshore rocks.

Tufted puffins range from northwestern Alaska to southern California; in Oregon they're estimated to be the sixth most common nesting seabird, with a population of about 5,000. They're also considered the most sensitive of Oregon's seabirds to intrusion or disturbance by humans or land mammals.

Nesting puffins burrow in soil atop islands or in sandy bluffs above beaches. The female lays a single egg in early May; after the chick hatches, about six weeks later, it spends six to eight weeks in the burrow, daily gobbling a dozen fish delivered by both parents.

Puffins prefer the seclusion of offshore rocks such as the two Haystack Rocks—at Cannon Beach and Pacific City—and the eastermost rock at Three Arch Rocks, site of the state's largest puffin colony, with an estimated 2,000 to 4,000 birds. They also nest on the mainland at a few isolated sites, including Heceta Head, the cliffs at Sea Lion Caves, Otter Crest, Cape Lookout, and possibly Cascade Head.

The best time to see tufted puffins is early in the morning during nesting season, from April through September; watch for short black wings flapping furiously as the birds fly in and out from the nest. The best places to see them in Oregon are (north to south) Haystack Rock at Cannon Beach, Yaquina Head, Cape Meares, the highway turnout just north of Sea Lion Caves, Heceta Head, and Coquille Point. In summer at Haystack Rock you may find members of the local Puffin Club setting up scopes to help visitors spot the birds.

6

Sand Lake to Neskowin

This stretch of coast just north of Cascade Head offers lots of quiet off-highway beach walking, as US 101 follows an inland route here, skirting Sand Lake and Nestucca Bay. Other than the bay mouth, sandy Cape Kiwanda is the only headland obstructing the beach, but it's easily ascended on foot. There are a few private campgrounds in the area and one Forest Service campground, Sand Lake. The beach and dunes around Sand Lake may not be very appealing for exploring on foot, however. Sand Beach Campground is

Steller's sea lions

principally used as a staging area for ORVs, which are allowed to range north from the campground to a point about halfway to Cape Lookout. They aren't allowed south of Sand Lake, however, and the lake's outlet can generally be forded at low tide in summer.

Beach walkers have only to decide how far they want to go and whether they're walking a return route or one way. In summer it's possible to walk on sand the entire distance from the base of Cape Lookout, past Sand Lake, over Cape Kiwanda, to Pacific City, even to Neskowin if you can arrange a boat shuttle at Nestucca Bay. More likely you'll walk only a portion of that, perhaps down Nestucca Spit and back in Bob Straub State Park. The beachside community of Tierra del Mar is a good place to begin a beach walk, heading north to Sand Lake and back or south over Cape Kiwanda and back. From Neskowin, near the base of Cascade Head, the

Sea Lions

Among the five species of pinnipeds (from the Greek word *pinna*, for fin, and the Latin *pedis*, for foot) found along the Oregon coast are two sea lion species: Steller's and California sea lions. Though similar in many ways, their migratory habits are quite distinct from each other. An awareness of each species' travels helps you understand what you're seeing and hearing, or know what to look for, while watching for marine mammals along the coast.

Steller's (northern) sea lions haul out at ten locations on the coast. Except for a year-round colony at Sea Lion Caves on the central coast, Steller's are summertime residents, arriving in the spring to breed at Rogue and Orford reefs on the southern coast and sometimes at Three Arch Rocks (as well as Sea Lion Caves). Oregon's breeding population of Steller's sea lions is particularly important because it's currently one of only two reproductive colonies in the United States between southern California and Alaska. In 1990 the Steller's was listed as a threatened species under the federal Endangered Species Act; federal wildlife officials estimated the Oregon breeding population at 3,229 animals in 1991.

California sea lions are wintertime visitors, and only

beach stretches north almost 4 miles to the mouth of Nestucca Bay. For one-way beach hikes, consider walking from the beach just south of Nestucca Bay (see Section 6 of the Oregon Coast Trail chapter for access information) or from Nestucca Spit with a boat shuttle, heading south to Neskowin, or from Tierra del Mar over Cape Kiwanda to the dory-launching beach near Pacific City, just south of the cape.

Kayaking. Much of Nestucca Bay isn't in view of the highway, which makes it even more attractive for wildlife watching by sea kayak. If you venture out in winter, keep your eyes open for Canada geese; a population of the diminutive Aleutian goose winters in this area, which is why, in 1991, the federal government began acquiring land around the bay to establish Nestucca Bay National Wildlife Refuge. There's a boat ramp off the road from US 101 to

male sea lions come to Oregon. After spending the breeding season off California and Baja California, the males leave the females and pups behind and migrate north, showing up along the Oregon coast in October and leaving by May. At least 2,000 male sea lions winter here; another 6,000 to 8,000 move through Oregon twice a year on their way to and from the British Columbia coast. Unlike their quiet cousins the Steller's, California sea lions have a loud bark—one reason they were used as circus animals in an earlier era (they're still popular with zoos and oceanariums). Listen for their barks on a wintertime hike to Hart's Cove or between Sunset Bay and Cape Arago.

Good spots to see either kind of sea lion are at Sea Lion Caves (admission fee) or from the highway turnout just north of the caves on the central coast north of Florence, and at Cape Arago on the south coast. If both kinds are together on one rock (as they may be in spring or fall), how do you tell the difference? The Steller's is about three to four times the size of a California sea lion, for one thing, and the Steller's is lighter in color. The California sea lion also has a "sagittal crest," or large bump, on its forehead, contrasting with the rounder skull of the Steller's.

Pacific City, which gives boaters good access to the mouth of the bay if it's not too windy. Otherwise, put in at a boat ramp near where US 101 crosses the narrow southern end of the bay, about 1.5 miles south of the road to Pacific City.

Cape Kiwanda State Park

Unlike its sister capes to the north, Cape Kiwanda is made of sandstone. It's eroding much faster than the coast's basalt capes, but along the way the waves are shaping its cliffs into gorgeous ocher sculptures.

For the most dramatic views of the cape's tip, climb up the steep sand slope toward the western end of the cape. Old fencing attempts to keep the curious away from the most dangerous cliffs on top. This is not a through route to the north side of the cliff, however. To get through to the beach on the north, go back down to the

Dory-launching on beach at Cape Kiwanda

dory beach and follow the tracks up the gradual neck of the cape inland from the tip. Coming from the north, the route over the cape is quite obvious. If you're lucky you may get to watch dories launching or landing at the foot of the cape. This is the more heavily used of two sites on the Oregon coast where beach-launched motorized fishing dories still put in and take out; the other is at Cannon Beach, alongside Haystack Rock. The boats are generally launched on an outgoing tide. The process requires considerable skill: back the trailered boat into the surf, gun the engine so the dory slides off into the shallows, drive quickly up the beach and park, run back to the boat and begin pushing it out through the surf from the stern, and then, at the right moment, give one last shove, wriggle over the transom, grab the wheel, fire up the engine, and gun it out through the surf, keeping it perpendicular to the waves.

Mount Hebo

If you travel on US 101 through Tillamook County rather than on Three Capes Scenic Route, consider detouring east a few miles to 3,174-foot Mount Hebo in Siuslaw National Forest. From the community of Hebo on US 101, turn east onto State Highway 22 and immediately turn onto Forest Service Road 14; drive to Hebo Lake Campground or continue, past South Point, to Mount Hebo Campground near the summit. The 8-mile Pioneer-Indian Trail travels through widely varying terrain, including unusual Coast Range alpine rock gardens, and is especially inviting during the spring wildflower bloom.

7

Cascade Head

In earlier times, Cascade Head—like Neahkahnie Mountain to the north—served as a vision-quest site for indigenous people who lived near the banks of the Salmon River. Thanks to preservation efforts by both private and public agencies, its original magic remains. From the top of the head you get arguably the best view on the entire Oregon coast—and that's saying something. Trails on the head traverse old-growth forest as well as rejuvenating second growth. Bobcats roam the forest, Pacific giant salamanders—the largest salamanders in the world—creep along the alder-studded streambanks, Chinook salmon run up the Salmon River in the fall, and Oregon silverspot butterflies flit over the grassy headland in the summer. Hikers often see hawks circling in the wind or deer grazing on the open headland late and early in the day.

In 1966 The Nature Conservancy bought 300 acres of land at the headland's western tip, preserving unique prairie and rain forest habitat. But preservation of Cascade Head began much earlier. In 1934 Congress set aside nearly 12,000 acres stretching from the shoreline across US 101 into the Coast Range, and including the Salmon River Estuary, as an experimental forest; seven years later the 700-acre Neskowin Crest Research Natural Area was designated within the experimental forest as an undisturbed educational and research site. Then in 1974 Congress created the 9,670-acre Cascade Head Scenic Research Area, overlapping the experimental forest and the Conservancy's preserve and thereby protecting whole watersheds and forest ecosystems. Research in applied forestry continues within the experimental forest, but scientists are also using the forest to study forest and estuary ecosystems, various threatened animal species, and global climate change.

Canoeing and Kayaking. To explore the Salmon River Estuary, launch boats at Knight County Park, 2.5 miles from US 101 on Three Rocks Road. If it's a calm day and the tide is right, consider floating downstream toward the mouth, preferably following the tide back upstream to return. If it's windy, paddle upstream deeper into the salt marsh.

Hiking. Cascade Head's most popular hiking trail is one

View south from grassy Cascade Head

through The Nature Conservancy's preserve. Though it's open to the public, Conservancy representatives are rightfully protective of the preserve, preferring that mention of it be omitted from guide-books such as this one. In deference to those who are working hard to preserve the headland's unique ecosystem, be careful to leave no trace on a hike along the headland trail. In addition to ordinary trail etiquette (don't litter, don't pick any vegetation), leave your dog at home and walk only on the trail, tempting as it may be to stray. Certainly don't camp or build a fire on the headland.

Trailheads at both the southern and northern ends of the Conservancy's trail are accessible by car. For an easy out-and-back hike, start at the north trailhead and walk 1 nearly level mile to the summit knoll. Alternately, it's about 1.7 miles from the south trailhead to the south viewpoint. Most of the elevation change occurs between the north and south viewpoints. If you have a shuttle car available, the 3.5-mile hike from the north to south trailhead makes a wonderful one-way, mostly downhill hike.

The Nature Conservancy Trail, though rightfully popular, is only one of three trails on the head. On the headland's north side, a Forest Service trail to Hart's Cove leads through magnificent hemlock and Sitka spruce, crossing creeks on picturesque footbridges. The Forest Service has also built a 6-mile Oregon Coast Trail link crossing over the headland inland from the Conservancy's preserve. It's well worth walking to enjoy the old-growth and second-growth forest it traverses. Forest Service Road 1861 cuts across this trail at its high point; for a shorter one-way, downhill hike through

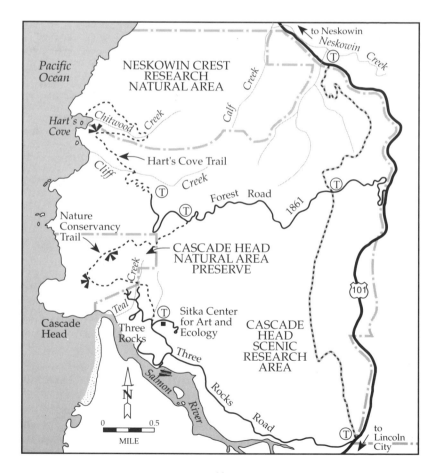

old-growth forest, leave a shuttle car at the south trailhead and hike only the 3.5 miles south from Forest Service Road 1861.

Cascade Head Oregon Coast Trail
6 miles, 1,120-foot elevation gain

The north trailhead is on the west side of US 101 about 2 miles south of Neskowin; there's room for a few cars to park here. The south trailhead is on the north side of Three Rocks Road at its junction with US 101, 1.3 miles north of State Highway 18; there's room for several cars.

From the north trailhead, the trail follows a fairly level route west along an old road, above a melodious creek, for 0.4 mile. Reaching a trail post, it veers left onto a narrower forest path and heads uphill. It continues up, gradually switchbacking or following the contours of the hill, alternating between old-growth hemlock, second-growth forest, deep Sitka spruce forest, and salmonberry-filled clearings. Nearing Forest Service Road 1861, it tops out, drops through an alder grove, and meets the road at 2.5 miles.

The trail resumes across the road about 50 yards to the west, immediately entering a lovely parklike ancient forest of hemlock, Douglas fir, and Sitka spruce. The trail follows the edge of a bog, filled with skunk cabbage blooming in March; then it crosses a creek on a footbridge and stair-steps through the bog on a boardwalk. After moving into second-growth forest, the trail seems to split about 2 miles from Forest Service Road 1861; bear left on the more well-worn path. Soon the trail begins switchbacking down the hill,

Shelf fungus on tree off Oregon Coast Trail

crossing creeks a few times, ending at the south trailhead 3.5 miles from Forest Service Road 1861.

Cascade Head Nature Conservancy Trail
3.5 miles, 1,200-foot elevation loss

The upper trailhead is 3.2 miles west on Forest Service Road 1861, which meets US 101 about 4 miles north of State Highway 18. The trail begins as an old road following the hillside's contours through deep, cool woods. After passing under a sign announcing your entry into The Nature Conservancy's preserve, you'll reach a signboard and kiosk with trail brochures at 0.6 mile. The trail emerges from the forest onto the grassy, open headland at 0.9 mile. From here it's a short walk to a benchmark signifying the summit knoll.

Continuing, follow the trail as it switchbacks down the west face to the south viewpoint at about 1.7 miles, near a line of fencing beyond which hiking is prohibited. The trail then curves west and follows a gently descending route back into the forest. It crosses several small creeks on wooden footbridges and boardwalks, then drops steeply down the hillside before ending at a roadside trailhead.

To reach the south trailhead by car, turn west off US 101 onto Three Rocks Road (2.7 miles south of Forest Service Road 1861, 1.3 miles north of State Highway 18) and drive about 2.5 miles to a fork at the county boat ramp. Bear right, up the hill, and continue 0.5 mile to the trailhead on the right, just past the entrance to Sitka Center for Art and Ecology.

Hart's Cove Trail
2.9 miles, 800-foot elevation loss

The trail starts at the end of Forest Service Road 1861, 0.9 mile past the northern trailhead for the Cascade Head Nature Conservancy Trail (see above). From the parking area, the trail switchbacks for 1 mile down to Cliff Creek and then ascends slowly as it follows the slope's contours north. A sign announces the trail's entry into Neskowin Crest Research Area; just beyond the sign there's a view of Hart's Cove. The trail then travels deep into a ravine, crosses Chitwood Creek at about 2 miles, and emerges from the forest at 2.9 miles. Stroll down the open slope to the south side of Hart's Cove for a view into it, but be aware that there is no way to get into the vertical-walled cove itself.

Boardwalk along Cascade Head Nature Conservancy Trail

Oregon Silverspot Butterflies

If you're wandering over salt-sprayed headland meadows on the northern half of the Oregon coast in the summertime, keep your eyes open for a medium-size orange butterfly flitting in the wind. It may be the Oregon silverspot butterfly, or hippolyta fritillary (*Speyeria zerene hippolyta*), an increasingly rare species specifically adapted to the rather harsh environment of the Oregon coastline.

The Oregon silverspot's range is the coastal strip from just north of the Columbia River down into northern California, though four or five of its six or seven primary sites are on the northern Oregon coast. Except at Mount Hebo in Tillamook County, the silverspot generally stays within a mile of the coast, frequenting open meadows touched by salt spray—the native coastal prairie atop Cascade Head, for example.

While members of some butterfly species all emerge into adult form within days of one another and live for just a few weeks, Oregon silverspots appear to emerge from the larval stage over a fairly long period and seem to have a longer than usual life span; they may be spotted anytime from July through September if conditions are right. This evolutionary strategy has helped the butterfly survive in the harsh coastal environment, with some individuals out mating or egg-laying almost all summer, regardless of conditions. A slight wind or even a cloud cover may keep other butterflies from flying, but not this one. If you spot an Oregon silverspot, notice how its body and the base of its wings, close to the body, are dark brown, unlike other orange butterfly species on the Oregon coast; biologists believe this coloration helps it absorb and retain heat where it's needed most. (The silver spots are along the underside edge of the wings; you can see them only if the butterfly is poised on a plant with its wings folded.)

Shrinking of its native habitat has caused the Oregon silverspot's numbers to fall, leading it to be listed as a threatened species. Industrial and residential development are partly to blame. Other factors include the spread of gorse, scotch broom, and other nonnative plant species; fire suppression that favors the growth of trees over that of open prairies; and simply more people doing more planting.

8

Lincoln City to Gleneden Beach

South of the Salmon River a low headland rises; then the terrain falls to flat beach stretching south nearly 10 miles, interrupted by the mouth of Siletz Bay at the south end of Lincoln City. With shops and restaurants strung along US 101, Lincoln City goes on for miles, much longer even than larger coastal towns. In fact, until residents voted to consolidate, it was actually a series of five communities. Now home to a large outlet mall, Lincoln City is busy with cars and shoppers year-round. The beach is busy, too, judging by the many kites visible in the sky from nearby US 101.

For a long beach walk, exit US 101 at the north end of town,

Salishan Spit

near the large Shiloh Inn motel, and follow signs west and north to Road's End State Wayside. From here you can walk north about 1 mile to the base of the headland, or south as long as you please, or until your progress is halted by the almost achingly narrow mouth of Siletz Bay.

Across the mouth lies Salishan Spit. The road up the spit is private, open only to homeowners and guests of Salishan Resort, but the beach here—as everywhere on the Oregon coast—is open to the public. It's accessible from Gleneden Beach Wayside just south of Salishan.

The U.S. Fish and Wildlife Service recently established a new national wildlife refuge at Siletz Bay and is in the process of acquiring lands around the bay for this refuge. A good spot to pause for some wildlife watching is at the public dock at the end of 51st Street, off US 101 at the south end of Lincoln City. Look for gulls, terns, and pelicans in summer and ducks, loons, and grebes in win-

The Oregon Beach Bill

In Maine, about 3 percent of the state's 4,000-mile coastline is public property. In Massachusetts, only 10 out of 1,300 miles of coastline are publicly owned. The story is similar in most coastal states. In Oregon, however, 262 miles of beaches and 64 miles of headlands are accessible to the public. That might not have been the case were it not for a remarkable and unique piece of legislation signed by Governor Tom McCall in 1967. However, the story of Oregon's Beach Bill really begins at the turn of the century with another visionary Oregon governor, Oswald West, if not centuries earlier, when the first coastal Indians ventured down the beach in search of food.

Elected in 1911, Governor West was an early and forceful advocate of preservation of open lands. To keep tidelands in public ownership while avoiding direct conflict with coastal landowners, West convinced the state legislature to designate all Oregon beaches a public highway, since there was, in fact, no other route along the coast. "I pointed out that thus we would come into miles and miles of highway without cost to the taxpayer," he later told a newspaper reporter. "The

ter. Harbor seals can be seen hauled out near the water's edge across the channel from the dock year-round.

About 1.5 miles to the south, just south of where US 101 crosses Drift Creek, there is a long dirt turnout on the west side of the highway. From fall through spring this is a good place to see large concentrations of Canada geese, ducks, and shorebirds, plus peregrine falcons and bald eagles.

The stretch of coastline from Lincoln City to Gleneden Beach is rather extensively developed, with lots of motels. There is only one public campground, at Devil's Lake State Park.

Devil's Lake

At the north end of town is Devil's Lake, a center of summertime activity, with boaters, swimmers, and sailboarders sharing the water. There are two state parks on the lake: on the west shore is

legislature and the public took the bait—hook, line and sinker."

West's legislation protected beaches only up to the high-tide line, however. As real-estate interests began focusing more attention on the coast in the 1960s, it became apparent that more action was needed to establish public ownership of the entire dry-sand beach. After several citizens complained to the state in July 1966 about being denied access to a portion of the beach in front of Cannon Beach's Surfsand Motel, a state parks advisory committee began examining the issue. Seven months later the committee approved the Beach Bill and it was presented to the state legislature; within five months it was passed by the legislature and signed into law by Governor McCall.

In essence, the bill recognized that, through frequent and uninterrupted use of the ocean shore, the public had long ago established its right to use the beach freely. The Oregon Supreme Court agreed, after the owner of the Surfsand Motel challenged the law. The public had acquired rights to use the beach under the common law doctrine of implied dedication, the judges said; the Beach Bill simply codified already existing public rights.

Long-tailed kite on beach at Lincoln City

Devil's Lake State Park, which has a campground (reservations accepted in summer), and on the south shore is East Devil's Lake State Park, a day-use area.

Canoeing. It's hardly a remote getaway, but canoeing can be pleasant on the long lake. Especially early or late in the day, you can glide quietly along the lake shore watching for birds, including bald eagles. You can expect to see lots of coots and ducks, and perhaps some loons, cormorants, and grebes, in the fall, winter, and spring months. Take along your own canoe and launch it at East Devil's Lake State Park or any of three boat launches on the west shore, one of them southwest of the campground where the lake narrows toward its outlet at the D River. Campers with canoes can also use a boat dock accessible by trail from the campground. You can also rent a canoe—or pedal boat, electric pedal boat, or bumper boat—at Blue Heron Landing, on the lake's northwest finger.

For swimming—in water substantially warmer than the Pacific Ocean—try Sand Point Park, north of East Devil's Lake State Park. Sailboarders use the park's sandy beach as well.

9

Lincoln Beach to Moolack Beach

*B*etween long, sandy Lincoln Beach and long, sandy Moolack Beach the coastline is rocky with no accessible beaches of any significance. Cape Foulweather is the most prominent headland in this stretch; a wayside at its tip (just off US 101) is a good vantage point for whale watching. Captain James Cook gave the cape its name on March 7, 1778—a particularly inclement day, apparently—during his voyage along the northern Pacific coast.

Depoe Bay, north of Cape Foulweather, is a tourist town situated on what residents claim is the world's smallest harbor, and it's quite a charming sight on a clear evening with the fishing fleet bobbing in the harbor. Because of the port's proximity to the open sea, charter boat operators in Depoe Bay are able to offer whale-watching tours as short as an hour, convenient—and inexpensive—for many travelers on the move. With the growing population of year-round resident gray whales off the Oregon coast, your chances of spotting a whale from one of these tours are good nearly any day.

The seawall along the highway here is more alarming than charming when a sou'wester is blowing, tossing seawater up onto US 101, but it's a popular spot to watch for whales, seals, and birds from land. No binoculars? Drop a coin into one of the telescopes arrayed along the seawall.

Storm-watching through coin-operated binoculars at Depoe Bay seawall

Fogarty Creek State Park, at the south end of Lincoln Beach, is an excellent place to picnic out of the wind, especially for families with children. The park is on the east side of US 101. Picnic tables are scattered along Fogarty Creek, which is spanned by several arching wooden footbridges. Asphalt paths on either side of the creek lead under US 101 to a pocket beach. Drivers approach the park from either of two unconnected access roads, both signed on US 101—one on the north side of the creek and the other on the south side.

There are no hiking trails on this part of the coast. Instead you'll find some of the best bird watching and tidepooling on the entire coast.

Boiler Bay State Park

This state park, which isn't much more than a wayside viewpoint, is known not only as as a very good place to watch for migrating gray whales, but as one of the best sites in Oregon from which to observe pelagic birds from land. Among the unusual species spotted here are various shearwaters, jaegers, Laysan albatrosses, and Clark's grebes, as well as more common birds, such as brown pelicans from August through October, Pacific loons in fall, and black oystercatchers year-round. It may also be the best site in Oregon to see marbled murrelets in spring and fall; you may even spot the rare ancient murrelet in winter. For the best birding, park at the west end of the wayside with binoculars or a spotting scope.

There are excellent tidepools just north of Boiler Bay, formed on bedrock shelves and between boulders. Access is a little difficult, however. Park at Boiler Bay State Park and walk (very carefully) 0.1 mile north along US 101 to a little scramble trail that drops down the cliffs next to a small, weathered commercial building. Boiler Bay is a state-protected intertidal area, with collection of invertebrates allowed by permit only.

Otter Crest–Devil's Punchbowl

Otter Crest is one of the most popular tidepooling areas on the Oregon coast. It's vast, with pools forming on wide, flat slabs of bedrock. Its popularity has led to its designation as a state "marine garden," which prohibits the collection of any critters. Evidence of overuse by enthusiastic visitors is easy to see, beginning with rocks once covered with barnacles that are now worn smooth by shoes. Do your best to limit your impact (see Chapter 10) if you visit the

Otter Crest tidepools, or consider scrambling down to the Boiler Bay tidepools as an alternative. The 0.1-mile trail to the beach here starts just inland from Devil's Punchbowl; park near the restrooms and follow the asphalt path.

The name Otter Crest refers to the shoreline in this area; it derives from Otter Rock, a small rock about 0.5 mile offshore (and now also the name of the community here). Otters once inhabited the waters around the rock, as they did much of the coastline; history records that this is also the site where, in 1906, the last remaining sea otter in Oregon was shot.

The viewpoint for Devil's Punchbowl is at the end of the road to Otter Rock. The bowl was formed with the collapse of the roof over two intersecting sea caves in the sandstone just offshore. At high tide, water enters the bowl and churns wildly. It's most dramatic during winter storms.

Opposite the public restrooms, stairs lead south down the cliff

Winding stairway to beach from Devil's Punchbowl

to the beginning of Moolack Beach, which is unobstructed as far as Yaquina Head, more than 4 miles to the south. Beverly Beach State Park is located near the north end of Moolack Beach.

Otter Crest and Devil's Punchbowl are located off Otter Crest Loop Road. Watch for signs along US 101 about 8 miles north of Newport or 5 miles south of Depoe Bay.

Beverly Beach State Park

Located 7 miles north of Newport and within a few minutes' drive of the Oregon Coast Aquarium, Yaquina Head, and other prime attractions on the central Oregon coast, Beverly Beach State Park (reservations accepted in summer) is a popular base camp for vacationing families. And it's no wonder—there are more than 200 tent and trailer sites. The campsites are strung along the north side of Spencer Creek, the farthest of them lying about 0.75 mile from the ocean and the closest sites just under the highway overpass from the waves. When choosing a site, you may have to balance noise from US 101 against proximity to the beach. A nature trail follows the south shore and part of the north shore of Spencer Creek, crossing it with two footbridges.

Waves

Waves begin with the wind, though not necessarily with the wind blowing in the immediate vicinity of the coast. More often, waves are the result of swells originating hundreds or even thousands of miles at sea. As wind blows over the surface of the ocean, it creates friction as it transfers its energy from the air to the water. That friction gets particles of water on the sea's surface turning in a circular orbit, rolling forward in the direction of the wind and then back under the sea's surface in a rolling motion. The height of each swell is equal to the diameter of that orbit.

Waves, as beachgoers know them, take their crested shape as the swells approach the shore. Here the bottom of a wave's internal orbit begins to drag on the ocean floor, creating an elliptical orbit rather than a circular one and shortening the distance between waves, making them steeper. At this

Waves roll onto Lincoln Beach north of Fishing Rock

point, friction with the seabed causes the wave to basically trip. The wave front hollows out as the depth of water decreases, until finally the cresting wave crashes onto the beach. And despite what you may have heard, the seventh (or the ninth, or the tenth) wave isn't necessarily the largest; in fact, there's no way to predict an individual wave's height.

Sometimes crashing waves leave great gobs of seafoam scattered across the beach. It looks like soap suds, but it actually signifies a healthy ocean. Salt and remains of dead microscopic plants in the water are whipped together by strong wave action to create the foam. In the summer, northwest winds and the earth's rotation move warm surface water offshore, replacing it with cold water from the deep. The rising water brings nutrient-rich "fertilizer" to the ocean's surface, nourishing the plankton living there. The plankton multiply and, together with the decaying plant matter, get stirred into the mix, which is why summer's sea foam can look especially dirty.

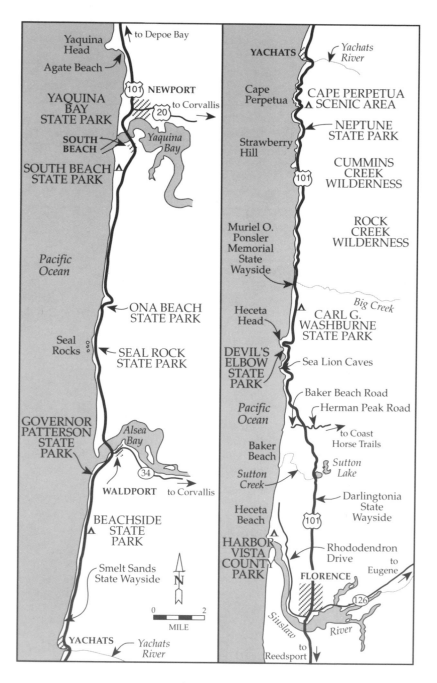

Opposite: *Salt marsh at edge of Yaquina Bay*

The Central Coast

10

Yaquina Head and Yaquina Bay

From its earliest days, Newport has been a popular tourist destination, and that aspect of the town hasn't changed. The town is bustling, both along the US 101 strip and on the old bayfront. There's plenty of lodging, from B&Bs to a large condominium complex facing the bay. Entertainment options range from classical concerts at the town's performing arts center to the bayfront wax museum.

Just north and south of town, however, it's easy to escape into relative wildness. Beaches stretch north and south from the bay mouth, and the bay itself offers excellent bird watching. Yaquina Head, north of town, has some of the best bird watching and tidepooling on the coast. And nestled nearly together in South Beach are two excellent interpretive centers offering close-ups of a large number of Pacific Coast creatures.

Yaquina Head Outstanding Natural Area

Yaquina Head was formed by Miocene-epoch lava flows; its hard volcanic basalt has endured the eroding effects of wind and waves while softer rock around it crumbled into the ocean. That basalt was also the landform's undoing, however; from 1925 to 1983 the area was quarried for local building and road construction material. The scars are still plainly visible on the 1-mile drive out to the tip of the head from US 101, about 2 miles north of Newport. Quarrying was halted three years after the Bureau of Land Management (BLM) took over the head in 1980, when Congress created Yaquina Head Outstanding Natural Area, and efforts are currently under way to develop some of the area's excellent wildlife-watching opportunities.

The headland is outstanding in many ways. From an observation platform built west of the Yaquina Head Lighthouse, you get some of the closest mainland views of a seabird colony in the United States from spring through midsummer. Among species nesting here are common murres, western gulls, Brandt's cormorants, and pigeon guillemots. Tufted puffins nest on the seaward side of the rock, though you may see them flying to and from their nests. Brown pelicans can usually be seen in the area in summer

Twenty-four-rayed sea star and photographer below Yaquina Head

and fall as well. From December to mid-May the platform is a good spot for whale watching. Even if you've come without binoculars or aren't interested in bird watching, the views north and south are stupendous.

There are tidepools just south of Yaquina Head along Agate Beach, but the truly outstanding tidepooling is at the end of the headland below the lighthouse, at the bottom of the wide wooden

Fish carcass above tidepools at Yaquina Head

staircase that rambles down the cliff to the rocky beach. Along the way, interpretive signs describe what you may see—seals, sea lions, gray whales, and intertidal creatures. (The BLM is hoping to build a new staircase here, perhaps in 1994, that will incorporate a view-point accessible to people in wheelchairs.) Harbor seals lounge on close-in rocky islands year-round, accompanied by their pups in spring, but don't get too close; all the islands are off limits as part of Oregon Islands National Wildlife Refuge. The tidepools here are a state-designated "marine garden," with collection of any animals found here prohibited. It also means it's particularly important to avoid disturbing the tidepools as much as possible, since this frag-ile environment gets lots of visitors.

Most unusual—perhaps even unprecedented around the world—is construction of a brand-new wheelchair-accessible tide-pool area in what was the lower quarry. Creation of a new intertidal area is itself novel enough. The first step was to excavate the area further, since the lower quarry was an average of 8 to 9 feet above sea level. Where workers didn't reach bedrock, huge boulders were imported to help create more habitat area. The next, more challeng-ing step is to design and build wheelchair-accessible paths and/or ramps into the intertidal area. These paths will be under water part of every day, so they must not only withstand the pounding of waves and the corrosive effect of seawater, but must resist col-onization by barnacles and other intertidal creatures. Some very high-tech materials may be used in the process, along with some not-so-high-tech materials, such as rubber. The area has been closed during excavation and construction, but it is scheduled to be com-pleted and open to visitors by fall 1994. There won't be too much to see at first, however; it will take time for intertidal creatures to slowly colonize the pools and rocks.

Other than the hiking you may do up and down the stairs to the tidepools, the only hiking opportunity at Yaquina Head is a short viewpoint trail. Look for red-tailed hawks, kestrels, and pere-grine falcons soaring overhead.

Yaquina Head Summit Trail
0.3 mile, 160-foot elevation gain

The trail starts directly behind the BLM field office at the east end of the Yaquina Head parking loop (1 mile west of US 101 on Lighthouse Road, about 2 miles north of Newport). The trail gradu-ally switchbacks up the steep hillside, ending with broad views to the north and south.

Yaquina Bay State Park

The 1871 Yaquina Bay Lighthouse, the only wood-frame lighthouse left in Oregon, is the centerpiece of Yaquina Bay State Park, just north of the bridge in Newport. It was used for only three years as a combination keeper's quarters and light tower until a more effective lighthouse was constructed just 3 miles to the north at Yaquina Head. It was scheduled to be razed in the mid-1940s until local citizens persuaded the state to preserve the structure. Drop by any summer day between 11:00 A.M. and 5:00 P.M., or weekends from noon to 4:00 P.M. the rest of the year, to see the restored and period-furnished lighthouse, which now also houses a gift shop. A trail steps down the steep hillside to the beach near the mouth of the bay; from here you can walk 3 miles north on the beach to the foot of Yaquina Head.

Yaquina Bay

Newport's bayfront is thoroughly developed, with plenty of cafes, galleries, and shops of all stripes. There's plenty to see outside as well, however. Public docks provide views of sea lions and harbor seals—too many, it may be argued; the animals sometimes congregate in such large numbers on the docks that they've caused entire docks to sink, fueling debate over the wisdom of extending the provisions of the Marine Mammal Protection Act of 1972. On the bayfront, look up as well as out for various gull species and other seasonal bird populations. The Mark O. Hatfield Marine Science Center sometimes offers naturalist-led dock walks along the bayfront (see below) and can provide information on charter-boat and airborne whale-watching trips out of Newport, Depoe Bay, and other points along the coast.

The south jetty can offer good bird watching along with views of seals and sea lions swimming in the channel between the jetties; orcas are sometimes spotted in the channel in early summer. Look for large congregations of scoters just west of the bridge from September through early May, as well as a great variety of ducks in the wintertime.

The *Oregon Coast Aquarium* opened at South Beach in 1992. Rather than attempting to display examples of marine habitats from around the world, its sole purpose is to introduce visitors, particularly children, to the varied life forms found at the Pacific's edge in Oregon. Inside a 40,000-square-foot building, live tanks represent four varieties of coastal habitat: wetlands, sandy shores, rocky shores, and offshore waters; perhaps most unforgettable is a tall cylindrical tank undulating with ghostlike jellyfish. Outside, interconnecting exhibits replicate scenes found along the coast, complete with machine-induced waves crashing among realistic-looking concrete rocks. Among the rocks, visitors meet such coastal residents as tufted puffins and rhinoceros auklets in an aviary, harbor seals and sea lions, and barnacles, mussels, and sea anemones continuously splashed by seawater in mock tidepools. The seabird exhibit is exceptional, giving visitors views they could never get from a headland overlook, such as an opportunity to see tufted puffins swimming underwater. Admission is charged.

The *Mark O. Hatfield Marine Science Center,* adjacent to the aquarium, has moved out of the spotlight since the aquarium opened next door, but it's still a wonderful place for families to visit and will be even more interesting after a planned renovation is completed in 1995 or 1996. In contrast to its neighbor, the center is primarily a research facility, and its aquarium exhibits currently are smallish and not as dramatic as the Oregon Coast Aquarium's realistic displays; but they hold a great variety of sea-dwelling species. Older children tend to appreciate the exhibits here more than do young ones, who enjoy the more hands-on approach of the Oregon Coast Aquarium. There's also a complete whale skeleton on display. The science center's shop is a good place to pick up books on coastal topics. The planned remodeling is designed to turn the public area into a state-of-the-art research and interpretive center, demonstrating why and how the ocean is studied. Admission is currently free (donations appreciated), but an entrance fee will be charged after the renovation.

For years the science center has presented Seatauqua, a series of educational classes and guided trips offered year-round, though concentrated in summer, in cooperation with the Oregon Department of Fish and Wildlife and other state, federal, and private agencies. Classes cover topics ranging from prehistoric fishing techniques to natural history of the rain forest. Some are for adults; others are oriented toward families and children. Call 503-867-0246 to find out what the current year's plans are.

Next to the science center there's a paved trail following the edge of the estuary, surveying a scene that changes constantly with the tides and the seasons. It's a good place to spot shorebirds during spring and fall migrations.

Hatfield Science Center Estuary Trail
0.5 mile

From the south end of the Yaquina Bay Bridge at South Beach, follow signs to the Mark O. Hatfield Marine Science Center. The trail begins at the east end of the science center parking lot. Here a paved trail begins winding along the edge of Yaquina Bay. It passes interpretive signs, which describe the dynamics of the estuarine system and identify many of its inhabitants, and two observation shelters facing the bay.

Respectful Tidepooling

Nearly three-quarters of Oregon's coastline consists of sandy beaches, but within and between those beaches are dozens of places where, twice a day, an ebbing tide reveals pools created by bedrock or boulders and filled with a particular variety of plants and animals adapted to the rhythm of the tides. Tidepooling can be like a treasure hunt as you search for familiar and unfamiliar creatures clinging to rocks or darting across pools.

Unfortunately, many of Oregon's tidepools are being loved to death. Often the first thing to go is the barnacles, simply rubbed off rocks from the tramping of many feet. Collecting intertidal animals is prohibited at four state-designated "marine gardens"—Haystack Rock, Otter Rock, Yaquina Head, and Cape Perpetua—and prohibited to all but researchers with a permit at four others—Boiler Bay, Strawberry Hill, Sunset Bay–Cape Arago, and Harris Beach. These are also the most popular spots for visitors, in part because they're easy to reach; to help preserve these overused areas, scan this book's chapters for suggestions of less well known tidepool areas. To help minimize disturbance to intertidal areas without giving up the treasure hunt entirely, keep the following in mind:

- Walk on well-worn pathways through the intertidal area, to avoid walking on any living plants or animals.
- Don't pick up any rocks. If you inadvertently move a rock, carefully and slowly put it back exactly as you found it. Sea urchins and sea anemones are particularly dependent on the shade of rocks and shells to keep them from drying out, and other plants and animals need ex-

The trail originally ended at a wooden pier stretching over a tidal marsh, but the pier now spans the marsh, granting pedestrian access to the Oregon Coast Aquarium. To reach the aquarium, cross the bridge and follow a short gravel path to a service road. Turn right and walk 0.1 mile, bearing left on an access road into the aquarium parking lot. To return to the science center, either return as you came (on the trail), or cross the service road and follow OSU Drive (walking in the bike lane) north to the science center parking area.

posure to light and food and will die if the rock they are on is overturned.

- Refrain from picking up any animals for a closer look, especially those clinging to rocks. If you do pick up an animal—a hermit crab, for example—put it back exactly where you found it. If it had been under cover, cover it again to protect it from exposure. If children in your party just have to touch something, take them to the Oregon Coast Aquarium or Mark O. Hatfield Marine Science Center in Newport; both have tanks designed for this purpose.
- If, where allowed, you gather any shellfish to eat, observe state fish and game regulations, usually posted at the site. Refrain from any collecting; the live plants and animals you take can't survive away from shore, and empty shells are recycled by hermit crabs, which need them for protection.

The best time to tidepool is during the hour or so on either side of low tide, and the best tides for viewing the widest variety of intertidal creatures are those of 0.0 feet and lower, called "minus tides." (To avoid harming the fragile creatures in the low-tide zone, avoid minus tides when taking school groups tidepooling, however.) The lowest daytime tides of the year generally occur in June and July. Morning low tides are better than afternoon ones because there's generally less wind to ruffle the surface of the water.

Tidepool explorers can usually count on getting their feet wet. To avoid an unexpected swim, keep an eye on the ocean, watching for unusually big waves, and take care not to get stranded on a rock as the tide flows back in.

11

South Beach to Alsea Bay

The coastline between Yaquina and Alsea bays consists of nonstop sandy beach, except for a large basalt outcropping at Seal Rock. The highway is close at hand most of the way, however. Nonetheless it's a section that invites long beach walks.

South Beach State Park

South Beach State Park, about 1.5 miles south of the Yaquina Bay Bridge, has a large campground (reservations accepted in summer) and a day-use area with picnicking and quick access to the beach. You can walk north about 1 mile to the south jetty, or south on several miles of open sand. The park also offers off-beach walking on a couple of trails: Cooper Ridge Nature Trail, encircling the campground, and South Jetty Trail, which leads north from the day-use area through the dunes to the south jetty.

Currently, Cooper Ridge Nature Trail is a nature trail in name only; its numbered posts are being reclaimed by the forest and are no longer recognizable, and there's no brochure available with descriptions corresponding to the numbered stations. New posts are to be installed in the near future, however. Recently, directional signs were posted along the trail, making the once-obscure route easier to follow. It's a nice trail for campers to stretch their legs on, particularly on a hot day (when it's cool under the Sitka spruce) or in the evening.

South Jetty Trail lends itself to an excellent, easy loop hike of about 2 miles, following the trail north to the south jetty and then heading back on the beach, picking up a spur trail to return to the campground or day-use area. It's open to mountain bikers as well as hikers. This trail may soon be paved, enabling cyclists to ride from the campground all the way to the Oregon Coast Aquarium.

South Jetty Trail
1 mile

The south trailhead is at the South Beach State Park day-use area; the north trailhead is near the end of the road leading out to

Platform overlooking salt marsh on estuary trail along Yaquina Bay

the south jetty (you may have to look hard into the grassy dunes to see the sign marking the start of the trail here). This straightforward trail follows a north-south route just inland from the beach grass– covered foredune. Along the way it crosses three paved spur trails between the beach and the campground. If you're starting at the trail's north end, bear left at the junction just beyond the start of the trail; a right turn leads out to the beach.

Cooper Ridge Nature Trail

1.5 miles

Campers in South Beach State Park can walk through the campground to the northernmost beach access trail and head west, watching for the Cooper Ridge Trail sign on their right as they head toward the beach. Otherwise, hikers can reach the trail via the South Jetty Trail; take the northernmost campground spur trail and look for the Cooper Ridge sign as you near the campground.

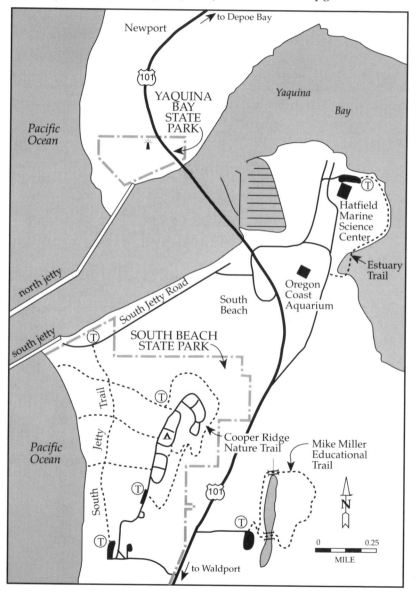

The trail heads up a sand dune and then quickly becomes a bit obscure; try bearing right to stay on top of the forested ridge. The route becomes clearer as it gains the ridge and begins circling the campground. At about 0.5 mile there's a bench with a nice view of the south jetty; a few minutes farther along, the trail drops down and passes a large anthill on the right, constantly under construction by a colony of *Formica formica* ants. The trail passes through a pine woods and meadow before climbing back up on the ridge. About when you start to hear the ocean again (about 1 mile), turn left at a junction to continue on the trail (going straight leads back into the campground) and proceed along the ridge until the trail ends near the registration booth at the campground entrance.

Mike Miller Educational Area

Just north of the entrance to South Beach State Park on US 101, a sign on the east side of the highway points the way to Mike Miller Educational Area. There, a loop trail originally built for use by school groups (but open to the public) leads through a variety of coastal forest habitats, including old growth, with huge stumps from long-ago logging, and blow-down. A "Forest Trail Guide" is available from the Lincoln County Parks Department; it's informative, but vandals seem to have removed numbers along the trail that would have corresponded to descriptions in the guide. A new trail guide and trail markers are planned.

Mike Miller Educational Trail
1-mile loop, 120-foot elevation gain

About 1.2 miles south of the Yaquina Bay Bridge on US 101, turn east at the sign to Mike Miller Educational Area; the gravel road goes straight a short distance and then swings right into a large parking area. Park and walk back to the trailhead, located where the road curves. Follow the trail uphill a short distance to where it splits into a loop; bearing left, the trail follows an old railroad bed for about 0.2 mile. It then veers right, drops down to cross the end of a long lake on a wooden boardwalk, and begins climbing through a Sitka spruce forest. The trail continues to climb slowly until it reaches the ridgetop, from which it slowly drops down to the edge of a blow-down area alongside a clearcut at about 0.7 mile; it then drops down to a long footbridge across the other end of the lake and completes the loop.

Ona Beach State Park

Ona Beach State Park is an outstanding day-use park, unassuming as it seems from the highway. It's at the mouth of Beaver Creek, where wintering birds can often be spotted. Picnic tables are scattered out of the wind and under the trees; from the parking area a footpath leads west over a gracefully arching footbridge to the beach.

Seal Rock State Park

Seal Rock State Park is a good place to see harbor seals and sea lions as well as various bird species year-round. In recent years the large monolith of columnar basalt at the shoreline has come to be known as Seal Rock, though that place name comes from Seal Rocks, a 2.5-mile-long ledge of partially submerged rock about 0.5 mile offshore. That's where the pinnipeds tend to lounge; carry binoculars for the best views. An asphalt path leads down the south side of the rock to the beach, where you can find bouldery tidepools out beyond the sand at low tide.

Hermit Crabs

Does every child remember the first time he or she held an empty-looking snail shell that turned out to harbor a hitchhiking hermit crab? Once past the shock of that first pinch, kids may find that hermit crabs are their favorite seashore creatures, easy to spot as they scamper across a pool, hauling their houses with them. They're also one of the most common types of crab found in Oregon's intertidal areas; look for them between or under rocks, or under masses of seaweed.

Unlike their well-armored cousins, hermit crabs have no hard covering over their soft, coiled abdomens, forcing them to curl into abandoned snail shells to protect themselves (though the claws that protrude from their "front doors" are tough enough). Eventually a hermit crab outgrows its shell and must find a new one, sometimes fighting other crabs for

Harbor seal

the right to occupy a particular shell if homes are in short supply. Once it finds a suitable shell, the crab stays put, leaving only when it's time to move into larger quarters. The most common type of hermit crab found in the midtide zone is *Pagurus hirsutiusculus*, whose name accurately attests to its obvious hairiness.

Hermit crabs are exemplary recyclers. When one hermit crab moves into a new shell, its old home is quickly occupied by a new resident, whose shell in turn is rapidly taken over by another hermit crab, and so on. Usually, the last move in a chain reaction like this is by a very small crab from a very dilapidated shell.

But to whom did the hermit crab's shell originally belong? Most often the crabs take up residence in shells from such common snails as *Nucella emarginata*, whose shell is pale, spiral-ribbed, and about an inch long. The smallest hermit crabs sometimes inhabit old periwinkle shells.

12

Waldport to Yachats

The beach on this stretch of coast is wide and long, with access at several points along the way, beginning with Governor Patterson State Park just south of Waldport. From here you can walk 7 miles south on unobstructed beach to the bottom of a small headland where the Yachats 804 Trail begins. The beach is the central recreational feature of this stretch of coastline; other than the blufftop Yachats 804 Trail, there are no hiking trails per se and no tide-pooling of note.

Among the beach access points are two public campgrounds. Beachside State Park is a relatively small state park campground (reservations accepted in summer); Tillicum is a relatively large Forest Service campground that tends to cater to motor homes more than most campgrounds in Siuslaw National Forest.

The Yachats 804 Trail is a short trail with a long history. It follows the proposed route of a county road that was never built. In the 1970s a group of local property owners filed suit to have the route vacated, to keep people from wandering between their property and the shoreline. Their suit eventually went all the way to the Oregon Supreme Court, which affirmed the county's ownership of the route. After the county transferred the land to the state parks division in the late 1980s, it was finally developed—but as a walking route and link in the Oregon Coast Trail rather than a road. Its compacted gravel surface makes it passable for wheelchairs.

The main trailhead is at its south end, at Smelt Sands Wayside, which has as its main attraction a long, wave-sculpted shelf of sandstone with a blowhole that, at high tide, shoots seawater with the pulse of the waves. It's great fun to explore, though it's slippery when wet and potentially dangerous during storms.

Yachats 804 Trail

0.75 mile

From the center of Yachats, drive north 0.5 mile and turn west at the sign to Smelt Sands Wayside. Follow the road 0.3 mile to a parking area and signed trailhead. Pick up the trail heading north along the bluff, overlooking a sandstone shelf. After passing a motel and some private homes, the trail leads into a stand of shore pines and skirts a narrow chasm at about 0.4 mile. Near the end it crosses Perch Street and drops down a sandstone bank to end at the beach.

Historic Alsea Bay Bridge Interpretive Center

The bridge crossing the mouth of Alsea Bay at Waldport is the newest of the coast's many bridges. It was completed in 1991 and replaces a 1936 bridge that had been considered one of the finest examples of concrete bridge construction in America, not only for its engineering but for such decorative features as its fluted entrance pylons and obelisk spires paired at the portal to the bridge's central arches. It was one of five major structures built as part of Oregon's Works Progress Administration–funded Coast Bridges Project and designed by state bridge engineer Conde B. McCullough (whose name is memorialized in the long bridge over Coos Bay just north of North Bend). Over the years the bridge deteriorated to the point where it had to be replaced, to the dismay of those who had successfully rallied to have it placed on the National Historic Register in 1981.

Exploring sandstone shelf along Yachats 804 Trail

To keep its memory alive, an interpretive center was built near the bridge's south end in Waldport. The center is small but intriguing and is open daily in summer (Wednesdays through Sundays in winter). Its primary mission is to educate the public about the old and new bridges and bridges in general, but those who arrange for displays and plan activities interpret that mission broadly, including nearly anything involving bridges and rivers. A ranger leads a daily bridge walk (weekends only in winter) and leads guided walks along the Yachats 804 Trail twice a week. Displays and activities are designed to appeal to people of all ages and may include anything from making a concrete bridge from a mold to take home as a souvenir to hands-on crabbing or clamming demonstrations.

Drift Creek Wilderness

About where Alsea Bay narrows to become the Alsea River, Drift Creek enters the river on its north bank. The creek is the centerpiece of Drift Creek Wilderness, a pocket wilderness of old-growth forest and streams flowing with steelhead and trout. A couple of trails cut through the wilderness leading to the creek itself, and more trails are being planned. For specific trail information, check in at the Waldport Ranger Station (see Appendix I).

Shore pines help define the landscape at Boardman State Park

Shore Pines

Ever wandered through a forest of ramrod-straight lodgepole pines high in the mountains? Those trees would seem to have little in common with the short, twisted shore pines you find growing atop sea cliffs or in sand dunes on the Oregon coast. In fact, they're two varieties of the same species—*Pinus contorta*—though botanists argued for years about whether they weren't actually two different species or, at least, subspecies.

Inland, lodgepole pines grow 50 to 100 feet tall, with a high crown of boughs clustered near the top of the tree. On the coast, shore pines average 25 to 30 feet in height, with a rounded crown of limbs sometimes begining at the ground. Wherever it grows, *Pinus contorta* is distinguished from other Northwest pines by its short needles, which grow in bundles of two, and its short (about two inches), round, hard, prickly cone. On the coast, shore pines may be found in either dry areas or bogs, and they're particularly common in the dunes of the central and southern Oregon coast. But their range is limited to the narrow (in places barely a mile wide) transition zone between the ocean and the start of the coastal forest.

Though they often grow in dense groves, it's not unusual to find a particularly contorted shore pine standing somewhat alone. This is known as a krummholz. Though one might assume it's been shaped mainly by blowing wind pushing vegetation to the tree's leeward side, in fact a krummholz generally has more foliage on its weather side, growing toward the rain, not away from it.

Some coastal Indians reportedly used the pitch from shore pines to help heal open sores and chewed the pitch or the buds to relieve sore throats; others used the tree's cambium layer to treat consumption or colds. Beyond that, the tree wasn't particularly useful to Indians, perhaps because of an ill-advised answer Pine gave to a query from those vain Younger Wild Women, according to the Nehalem Tillamook tribe. In a story related in *Nehalem Tillamook Tales*, when the women asked Pine what he thought of their looks, Pine didn't say anything complimentary, so they decided, "Pine, you will be good for nothing except merely burning."

13

Cape Perpetua to Big Creek

Cape Perpetua Scenic Area

With its craggy punchbowl-strewn shoreline, intriguing tidepools, dramatic vistas, and deep Sitka spruce forest, Cape Perpetua just south of Yachats is one of the most engaging areas on the coast. The cape is formed of layers of lava, which cooled into basalt and were uplifted millions of years ago. It was "discovered" and named by Captain James Cook in 1778, but shell middens found along what is now called Captain Cook Trail indicate that Alsi Indians discovered the cape much earlier, camping here and gathering shellfish in summers between about A.D. 600 and 1620.

Cape Perpetua and neighboring wilderness areas comprise the centerpiece of what a local grassroots forest preservation group has designated the Coastal Oregon Rainforest Reserve. The 85,000-acre area includes the largest intact forest canopy in the contiguous forty-eight states. Concerned about timber sales proposed for the forest in the early 1990s, this group of local residents and researchers successfully blocked those sales, keeping the forest intact. In the middle of the reserve is a 116-acre National Audubon Society sanctuary; plans call for construction of trails there in the future.

You could spend several days just exploring the Cape Perpetua area, camping perhaps in the Forest Service campground, which caters to tent campers and is arrayed along gurgling Cape Creek; listen for spotted, great horned, and pygmy owls in the campground. (RV campers may prefer larger Tillicum Beach Campground, another Forest Service campground about 7 miles north.) Begin by stopping at the visitors' center, which has well-presented displays dealing with local human and natural history. The bookshop sells books and maps, and large signs provide an overview of the area's trails. With its picture windows facing west, it's also a good spot from which to watch for whales during winter rains. The center is generally open daily in summer, weekends only in winter.

Plan lots of time at the shore, particularly at low tide. The bedrock shelves at the base of Cape Perpetua make for excellent

View south from Cape Perpetua's summit

tidepooling, and a ranger is frequently on duty, especially on weekends and in summer, to talk to visitors about what they see. No collecting of any tidal creatures is permitted. The tidepools, a state-protected "marine garden," are a short walk from the visitors' center (or from a turnout along the highway) via the Captain Cook Trail.

Farther south, the tidepools just south of Strawberry Hill, in Neptune State Park, are also exceptional; notice the mixture of columnar basalt and volcanic rock forming the pools. This is one of the better places to see harbor seals; they lounge on rocks barely separated from the mainland by a moatlike channel. You'll also find tidepools south about 1 mile between Bob Creek (where there is parking at a wayside) and Bray Point; pools set in a rock shelf here hold a nice variety of midtide zone plants and animals.

At high tide, both the Captain Cook Trail and the Trail of Restless Waters have surprises. Off Captain Cook Trail is the Spouting Horn, where a hole in the top of a sea cave at the end of Cook's Chasm spouts air and water when incoming waves build pressure inside the cave. The Trail of Restless Waters leads to Devil's Churn, another dead-end chute where waves rush in, smash a rock wall, and shoot seawater into the air. Hike either trail, or link them to make a 1.3-mile loop.

Forest Hiking and Mountain Biking. Inland, trails lead deep into coastal forest, much of it old-growth Sitka spruce. A good choice with young children is the 2-mile round-trip walk to the Giant Spruce; you can cut the whole walk to just 0.4 mile by starting at the end of the campground road rather than at the visitors' center.

You can drive to the top of the cape, where short Whispering Spruce Overlook Trail circles around for views. You can also hike to the top—or just hike back down—on Saint Perpetua Trail.

Several interconnecting forest trails offer opportunities for loop hikes. For a 2-mile hike, follow Cooks Ridge Trail to the start of a midtrail loop at about 0.7 mile (see map). Link Cooks Ridge Trail with Gwynn Creek Trail and a short section of the Oregon Coast Trail to make a 6.4-mile loop. For a 9.3-mile loop, join Cooks Ridge Trail with Cummins Creek Trail, plus a stretch of the Oregon Coast Trail and a 0.2-mile walk along the gravel Cummins Creek Trail access road.

Cummins Creek Trail is open to mountain bikers as well as hikers. For a scenic and moderately challenging loop, ride 4 miles up Forest Service Road 55 to the upper Cooks Ridge trailhead. Pick up the trail and follow it uphill another 0.2 mile and then bear left onto Cummins Creek Trail. It's a steep, tricky descent for about 1.3 miles, then an easy 3.2-mile cruise along an old roadbed to the lower trailhead. Ride out to US 101 and head west along the highway back to your starting point.

Trail of Restless Waters
0.7 mile

From the Cape Perpetua Visitor Center, follow the main trail west under the highway (or, from the adjacent highway turnout, take the footbridge and path west). At the trail junction, bear right.

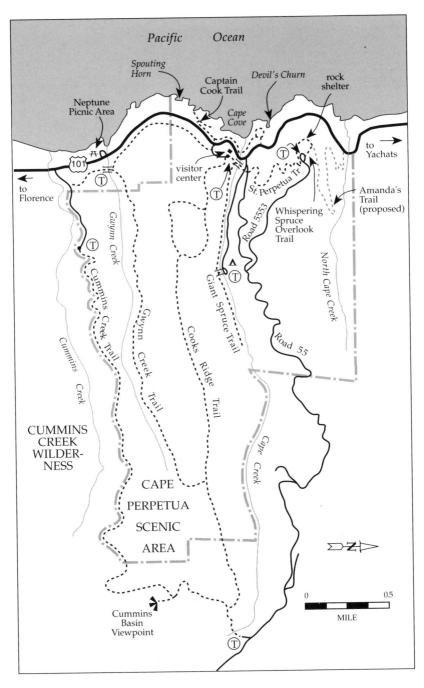

Landmark at end of Giant Spruce Trail

The trail leads north a bit, then heads back up to the highway, follows its shoulder a short distance, and resumes as a footpath down the hill. After passing a spur to Cape Cove, the trail soon meets the start of a short loop leading to Devil's Churn. To return from Devil's Churn, continue on around the loop (which leads up to the Devil's Churn parking area and back into forest), or simply retrace your route.

Captain Cook Trail
0.6 mile

From the Cape Perpetua Visitors' Center, follow the main trail west under the highway (or, from the adjacent highway turnout, take the footbridge and path west). At the trail junction, bear left. A second junction marks the start of a loop; bearing left, it first leads past Spouting Horn and then to tidepool access.

Giant Spruce Trail
1 mile, 140-foot elevation gain

From the Cape Perpetua Visitors' Center, follow the asphalt path down to Cape Creek, but rather than cross the creek, walk up its south bank. You'll pass a second footbridge at 0.8 mile (it leads to the end of the campground road); from here it's 0.2 mile to the trail's namesake, a huge, 500-year-old Sitka spruce.

Whispering Spruce Overlook Trail
0.25-mile loop

From the Cape Perpetua Visitors' Center, drive north a short distance on US 101 and turn east up Forest Service Road 55; then turn left onto Forest Service Road 5553, which leads to the cape's summit. This short, partially paved path loops around the summit, linking Saint Perpetua Trail and the proposed Amanda's Trail. The rock shelter on the west side, built in 1933 by the Civilian Conservation Corps and used as a Coast Guard lookout during World War II, is a good spot for whale watching.

Saint Perpetua Trail

1.5 miles, 600-foot elevation gain

From the Cape Perpetua Visitors' Center, follow an asphalt path down to Cape Creek, cross the creek, and continue across the campground road and Forest Service Road 55. Steep at first, the trail switchbacks through forest up the cape's south side. About 0.2 mile from the top, a spectacular view opens to the south. Continue up the grassy hillside to the rock-walled viewpoint at the top (accessible by car).

Cooks Ridge Trail

3.7 miles, 1,200-foot elevation gain

From the Cape Perpetua Visitors' Center, walk to the trailhead at the upper end of the parking lot. The trail begins in dense Douglas fir and spruce and then leads into old-growth Sitka spruce at about 0.7 mile, where a 0.6-mile midtrail loop begins. Hike the loop and return as you came, or continue up the trail beyond the loop, slowly ascending Cooks Ridge through mixed old- and newer-growth forest. After 2.4 miles, the trail meets the top of Gwynn Creek Trail. It continues gently up and meets the top of Cummins Creek Trail at 3.5 miles and then ends at Forest Service Road 55. The upper trailhead is 4 miles up Forest Service Road 55 from US 101.

Gwynn Creek Trail

3 miles, 1,200-foot elevation gain

The trail begins off the Oregon Coast Trail, 1 mile south of the Cape Perpetua Visitors' Center. Walk to the trailhead from the visitors' center on the Oregon Coast Trail, or park in the wayside off US 101 about 1 mile south of the visitors' center, cross the highway, walk around the gate and up a grassy clearing, and look left for the footbridge crossing Gwynn Creek. The trail begins at creek level but immediately begins a slow climb up the hillside north of the creek through forest, much of it old growth. The trail crosses several side creeks; one at about 1.5 miles is especially pretty, cascading in a fan down a rock face. At about 2.5 miles the trail switches left, leading out of the protected valley and onto windier Cooks Ridge. The trail ends at its junction with Cooks Ridge Trail. Return as you came, back down Gwynn Creek Trial, or follow Cooks Ridge Trail 2.4 miles back down to the visitors' center for a loop hike.

Cummins Creek Trail
4.5 miles, 1,360-foot elevation gain

From US 101 about 1.3 miles south of the Cape Perpetua Visitors' Center, turn west at the sign to Cummins Creek Trailhead and drive 0.3 mile to the road's end. The trail follows an old road on a gentle uphill grade. It enters a beautiful grove of old-growth Sitka spruce at about 0.5 mile and continues up the old road, in and out of old growth, for 3.2 miles. Then the trail leaves the old road and

Marbled Murrelets

Think of old-growth forests, and what bird comes to mind? Anyone with even a passing familiarity with ancient-forest issues might think first of the spotted owl. But a secretive robin-size seabird is every bit as dependent on survival of the old-growth forest, specifically along the coast.

The marbled murrelet (*Brachyramphus marmoratus*), in the same family as puffins and murres, is found on the Pacific Coast from Alaska to central California. Like many birds, it was once common on the Oregon coast, but fragmentation of the old-growth forest (on which it depends for nesting) has reduced its numbers drastically. In 1992 it was listed as a threatened species; estimates put the species' total Oregon population at between 2,000 and 3,500.

What little is known about the marbled murrelet's nesting and breeding habits has mostly been discovered since about 1990. That's the year the first nest was found in Oregon (in the Siuslaw National Forest). As of January 1993 only forty-four marbled murrelet nests had been found anywhere in the bird's range, ten of them in Oregon.

Considering the bird's secretive habits, it's a wonder any nest has ever been found. In Oregon, marbled murrelets nest

bears left up a narrower, rockier, steeper footpath. At 3.8 miles a spur on the right leads 0.1 mile to a viewpoint overlooking a sea of trees in Cummins Basin. The trail continues up rather steeply to end at a junction with Cooks Ridge Trail, 0.2 mile from Forest Service Road 55.

Cummins Creek Wilderness and Rock Creek Wilderness

In 1984, Cummins Creek Wilderness, adjacent to Cape Perpetua Scenic Area, and Rock Creek Wilderness, a few miles south, were created to preserve some of the last major virgin stands of Sitka spruce, western hemlock, and Douglas fir in the coastal forest. Only one trail traverses Cummins Creek Wilderness; Rock Creek is virtually trailless.

exclusively on large mossy or duff-covered tree limbs in old, deformed conifers, usually anywhere from 150 to 200 feet off the ground. They nest in groups at least 40 miles inland, but they feed at sea on small fishes and invertebrates. Flying through the forest at more than 50 miles per hour, murrelets may make the trip from nest to ocean and back as many as five times a day when feeding young in the nest.

Don't count on seeing a marbled murrelet in the forest; they're small, quiet, and quick. You might hear one if you get up early enough; listen for a gull-like "keer-keer" cry on a daybreak walk in a coastal old-growth forest. You have a better chance of seeing one at sea, off major headlands and jetties, especially in fall and spring. In Oregon they're most common between Yaquina and Coos bays. Some of the best places to see them, reportedly, are the Tillamook Bay north jetty, the lighthouse at Cape Meares State Park, and Boiler Bay State Wayside. Look for a compact, robin-size bird with a large head, short neck, short wings, and a rapid wingbeat. Its upper parts are dark and its under parts are white; plumage is mottled brown during breeding. The marbled murrelet is easily confused with its relatives the rhinoceros auklet, pigeon guillemot, and common murre.

The only trail through Cummins Creek Wilderness is Cummins Ridge Trail, a 6.2-mile route whose lower 3.5 miles originated as a logging road in 1968. The road was closed to vehicles in 1984, and 2.7 miles of footpath have been added to the upper end to take the trail all the way to the road at the edge of the wilderness. Though it's a rather long drive to the upper trailhead, the upper few miles are the most appealing part of the trail, where it winds through the old growth on a narrow footpath; once the trail leads onto the old road, you feel somewhat walled off from the forest by the thick growth of alders on either side of the road-trail. With a shuttle car you could hike it one-way downhill.

Rock Creek Wilderness has no formal trails, and there are no plans to build any. However, one trail does lead a short distance out of Rock Creek Campground along the creek's north bank; in the summer, hikers in river shoes could continue wading up into the wilderness. The campground is very appealing for car camping; a handful of campsites are arrayed along the gurgling creek in lush forest. Look for signs of beavers along the creek on the road into the campground.

Across the creek from Rock Creek Campground a Forest Service hiker/biker camp is being developed. You can reach Lanham Bike Camp by foot on a short trail that leads east from US 101 on the south side of Rock Creek.

Cummins Ridge Trail
6.2 miles, 1,360-foot elevation loss

For a one-way, downhill hike, leave a shuttle car at the western trailhead and begin hiking at the eastern trailhead. To reach the

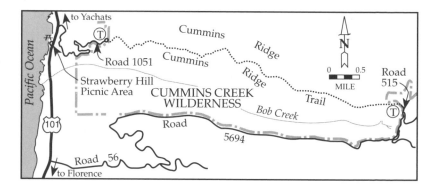

western trailhead from US 101, turn up Forest Service Road 1051 at the sign to Cummins Ridge Trailhead (2 miles south of the Cape Perpetua Visitors' Center road) and drive 2.2 miles to the trailhead end of the road. (The road actually continues northward a short distance, though it's narrow and virtually impassable to vehicles.) To reach the eastern trailhead, turn off US 101 on gravel Forest Service Road 56 just north of Tenmile Creek Bridge. At 2 miles, turn left onto paved Forest Service Road 5694. Continue straight on Forest Service Road 5694 where a spur road comes in from the right in 7.8 miles; shortly after the road turns to gravel, turn left on Forest Service Road 515 and follow it about 0.2 mile to where it ends at the trailhead.

From its eastern end, the trail begins as a narrow path through the woods, following the ridgeline. At 2.7 miles it leads onto an old roadbed, easy to follow and well maintained but somewhat brushy for lack of hikers. Watch as the predominantly Douglas fir forest slowly gives way to Sitka spruce as you near the coast. The trail continues on the old road all the way to the western trailhead.

Rock Creek Trail

0.2 mile

Follow the access road into Rock Creek Campground, about 8 miles south of the Cape Perpetua Visitors' Center. Just beyond where the road turns to gravel, beyond the campsites, a footpath takes off straight ahead, along the creek. It continues barely 0.2 mile before fading into the creekside brush, though hikers could continue into the wilderness by wading upstream.

Beaver-downed tree along Rock Creek

14

Heceta Head to Florence

For hikers, the stretch of coastline from about Big Creek to Florence is a transitional area between the headland and wilderness hiking available in the Cape Perpetua area and the low, undulating landscape of the Oregon Dunes National Recreation Area south of Florence. The dunes actually start just south of Heceta Head; from the headland south to the Siuslaw River's north jetty there's a long stretch of usually deserted beach, accessible either from the jetty (off Rhododendron Drive in Florence), from Sutton Beach Road, or from Baker Beach Road, which leaves US 101 where it flattens out south of the headland (rough trails lead about 0.5 mile through the dunes from the road's end to the beach). You may see horses on this stretch; a local horse outfitter leads rides out from Baker Beach, and another outfitter offers rides in a "stagecoach" pulled by Percheron draft horses beginning at the north jetty.

Emerging from forest into sunlight on Valley Trail

Carl G. Washburne State Park

The rather secluded beach on the north side of Heceta Head combined with trails on the east side of US 101 offer varied day-hiking opportunities at Carl G. Washburne State Park. Here the beach is shielded from the highway by forest; it's accessible at Muriel O. Ponsler Wayside, a beach access parking area for

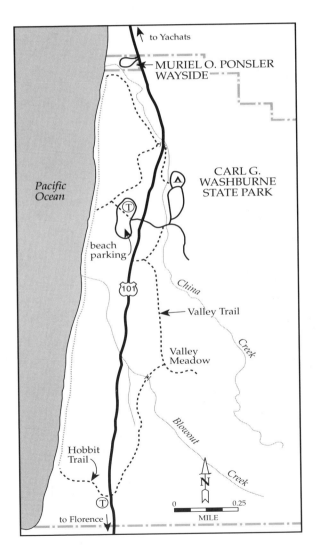

Washburne park, and via the 0.25-mile Hobbit Trail. Among the possibilities: a short walk to the beach on the Hobbit Trail, a slightly longer walk to an often sunny meadow on the Valley Trail, a one-way beach walk from one beach access to the other, or a 3- or 4-mile loop walk combining beach and forest walking.

The park's campground is open year-round but does not accept reservations. It is located about 13 miles north of Florence.

Hobbit Trail
0.25 mile, 200-foot elevation loss

The trail begins just across US 101 from a wide turnout on the east side of the highway (1.2 miles south of the entrance to Carl G. Washburne State Park, or 0.8 mile north of Devil's Elbow State Park); look for the trail mileage sign. Cross the highway and enter the woods where a wooden post marks the trail's start. The path winds gently downhill through a dense forest of pine, spruce, and tall rhododendron, closing in tunnellike near the end. It then opens up into a narrrow corridor of salal before ending at the beach just north of towering Heceta Head.

Valley Trail
1.6 miles, 120-foot elevation loss

The trail begins on the east side of US 101 at a trailhead shared with the Hobbit Trail (see above). It drops briefly and continues fairly level, following the route of the old coast highway along slow-moving Blowout Creek. At 0.5 mile the trail passes a couple of ponds; look for evidence of beavers. It crosses a creek and then continues north through the woods, suddenly emerging from the trees and dropping down into Valley Meadow at 1.3 miles. A side trail heads east a short distance, crossing China Creek. Continuing north on the main trail, the route climbs onto an old road lined with shore pines, meeting the road into Washburne State Park at 1.6 miles.

To make a 3-mile loop with the Hobbit Trail, follow the campground road west to US 101, cross the highway, and pick up the trail, which cuts across the parking loop at the park's beach access; then walk south 1.2 miles to the west end of the Hobbit Trail. To make a 4-mile loop, follow the paved campground road north to the end of the campground and pick up the paved path heading north. It leads under the highway along China Creek and emerges near the creek at the beach. Turn south and walk 1.7 miles on the beach to the end of the Hobbit Trail.

Sitka spruce reach out their limbs along Hobbit Trail

Devil's Elbow State Park

Devil's Elbow State Park, about 11 miles north of Florence, is a great place to spend a day at the beach, particularly with kids, because it has so much going on. The small, enclosed cove is fun for wading, but it's big enough to fly kites. Children enjoy "sailing" driftwood boats down Cape Creek, which empties into the ocean at the south end of the beach. To hike up the creek, follow a gravel road under the highway bridge, past a gate, and over a plank bridge spanning the creek. Immediately bear left on a trail that follows an old road alongside the creek another 0.6 mile or so to a wide elk pasture.

There's also a scenic, short hike up to Heceta Head Lighthouse, passing the white, Queen Anne–style light-tender's house (called Heceta House and now used for workshops and classes by Lane Community College). From the grassy flat at the base of the 1893 lighthouse, hikers can look east to watch for fishing boats, whales, or seabirds nesting on the offshore rocks, or look back west to watch the huge original Fresnel lens still turning slowly in the lighthouse tower.

Heceta Head Lighthouse Trail
0.5 mile, 120-foot elevation gain

From the north end of the parking area at Devil's Elbow State Park, follow the trail past picnic tables and up the hill. The trail fol-

Deer tracks in soft sand along Sutton Trail

lows the route of an old wagon road up the headland. At about 0.25 mile you pass the lighthouse-keeper's house; a spur trail leads east to a viewpoint overlooking Parrot Rock (so named in the late 1800s for the tufted puffins—"sea parrots"—that have since abandoned the island). Continue on the main trail another 0.25 mile to reach the lighthouse itself. Return as you came.

Sea Lion Caves

Just south of Devil's Elbow State Park is Sea Lion Caves, a commercial enterprise offering views into the largest sea cave in the world. The cave is home to a large colony of Steller's sea lions in fall and winter; in spring and summer the sea lions loll about on off-shore rocks, best seen from the highway turnout just north of the commercial development at the caves. The commercial hype at the caves is something of a turn-off, especially when the unavoidable gift shop is packed with visitors in midsummer, though a look inside the caves is still worth the admission price, at least once. You may see nesting pigeon guillemots or auklets inside the cave in spring and summer.

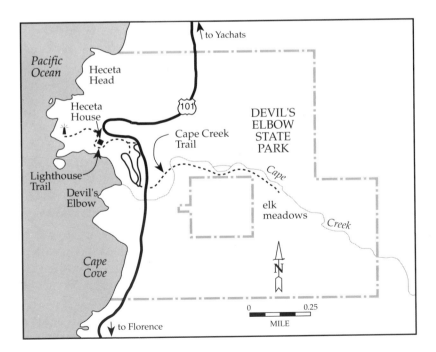

Darlingtonia Wayside

Darlingtonia Wayside, on Mercer Lake Road on the east side of US 101 just north of Sutton Beach Road, is not to be missed. A short asphalt path leads to a long wooden boardwalk overlooking a bog thick with the carnivorous plant *Darlingtonia californica*, better known as the pitcher plant, or cobra lily. Another Darlingtonia bog and overlook (wheelchair accessible) is located near the entrance to Sutton Campground.

Coast Horse Trail System

In 1993 the Forest Service completed construction of 14 miles of equestrian trails in the Cape Mountain area, in the mountains east of Baker Beach. Two trailhead sites, Horse Creek and Dry Lake, each have water for horses, holding corrals, and toilets. Among points of interest along the trails are a reproduction of an Indian *hitsi*, or log shelter, and the site of the 1932 Cape Mountain Lookout, where interpretive facilities may eventually be built. Access to the horse trail system is off Herman Peak Road, about 8 miles north of Florence. For more information and a map of the trail system, contact the Mapleton Ranger Station (see Appendix I).

Insect-eating Plants

Two species of insectivorous plants can be found in bogs on the southern half of the Oregon coast.

The greenish purple leaves of the pitcher plant (*Darlingtonia californica*) look a little like mustachioed cobras jutting up anywhere from six inches to three feet out of their crowded bogs. The leaves are what lure, capture, and digest the insects the plant uses to supplement its diet with nitrogen; bugs fly into the tubular, hooded leaves, are caught by a sticky secretion, and are digested by enzymes. The leaves are the most morbidly fascinating feature of Darlingtonia, but look also for the plant's nodding, purple flower topping a slender stalk during its blooming season, June through August.

Harder to spot is the much smaller sundew (*Drosera*

Darlingtonia
californica

rotundifolia). Its rounded leaf blades, fanned out close to the ground, are covered by fine hairs tipped with digestive glands. Insects get trapped in the hairs—and the rest is dinner. The plant's small, white flower blooms atop a two- to twelve-inch stalk in summertime.

The best place to see the pitcher plant on the Oregon coast is the Darlingtonia Wayside, on the east side of US 101 a short distance north of Florence. Nearby, a boardwalk viewing area at the entrance to Sutton Campground winds past another Darlingtonia bog, but it's not as thick (and, hence, not as impressive) as that at the Darlingtonia Wayside. To spot sundew along the trail at South Slough (see Chapter 18), pick up an Estuary Study Trail guide at the visitors' center and follow it to the sundew bog near the dikes at the trail's end.

Sutton Lake–Sutton Creek Area

Between campgrounds at Alder Lake and Sutton Creek there's an interesting and relatively little-used trail system that winds through forest, dune, and creekside habitats. With such outstanding hiking available to the near north and south, the Sutton Creek area can't compete as a destination day hike, but it provides wonderful opportunities for wildlife watching and quiet forest wandering for families camping in the area. Follow the meandering paths, watching for animal tracks in the sandy tread, or follow the trails to a rather remote stretch of beach.

At the end of Sutton Beach Road, Holman Vista has a wooden boardwalk and raised viewing platform (wheelchair accessible) overlooking the dunes and Sutton Creek estuary. Years ago beach-

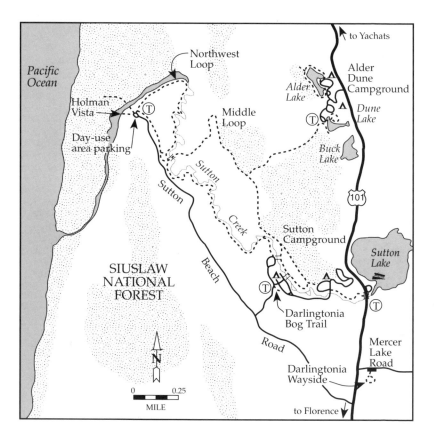

goers could cross the creek on big logs wedged in the creek bank just north of where Holman Vista is now, but they were eventually washed away during high water. Now you have to roll up your pant legs and wade to reach the beach from here, but this is easy enough in summer when the creek is low.

Sutton Trail System
6 miles (northwest loop, 1.5 miles; middle loop, 2.5 miles)

More a trail system than a single trail, Sutton Trails loop between Sutton Campground, Alder Dune Campground, Holman Vista and the Sutton Day Use Area, and Sutton Lake. The trails are mostly fairly level, though they climb and drop slightly in a few places. They traverse terrain ranging from dense forest to lush creekside meadows and pockets of open sand dunes. Trail junctions are generally clearly marked with destinations, though individual trails have not been named.

About 6 miles north of Florence, turn west on Sutton Beach Road. The road to Sutton Campground is on the right in about 1 mile; the road ends in another 1.5 miles at Sutton Day Use Area.

With a map (the one in this book, or photocopied maps available free at either campground) you can pick a route and head out for as long an outing as you like. Use the trails to walk to a lake to try the fishing or to take a dip, or to walk to the beach from your campsite. Or just follow a creekside route to see what you can see.

The trails may be accessed at any of several points, but the main trailheads are at Sutton Boat Launch, off US 101 north of Sutton Beach Road (the trail leads under US 101 along Sutton Creek); Sutton Day Use Area; Sutton Campground (two footbridges provide access to the trail across the creek); and Alder Dune Campground. The trail system includes a trail that circumnavigates Alder Lake.

The northwesternmost loop passing Holman Vista is about 1.5 miles long; the middle loop along Sutton Creek is about 2.5 miles.

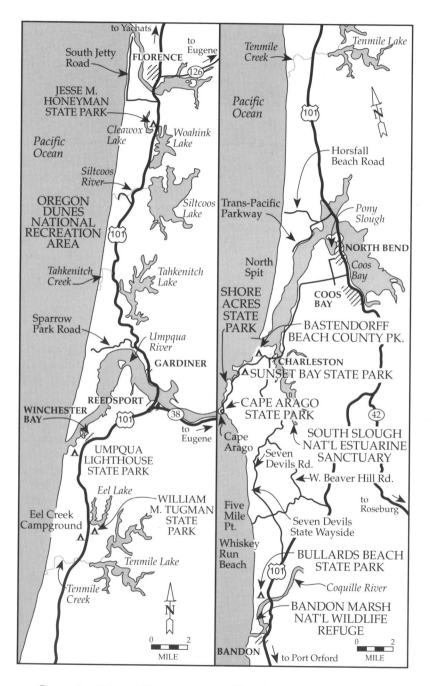

Opposite: *Hikers following posts marking Oregon Dunes Overlook Trail*

The South-Central Coast

15

Oregon Dunes: North

Oregon Dunes National Recreation Area

*S*tatistics tell part of the story of the Oregon Dunes National Recreation Area (NRA): it is the largest expanse of coastal sand dunes in the United States, with some dunes as tall as 500 feet. But numbers aren't adequate to express the essence of the dunes' appeal, which has more to do with the way light and shadow play across the sand and the expansiveness all that open sand represents—and inspires.

Footprints across Oregon Dunes

Hiking trails cross the dunes to the beach in several spots, though some hikers prefer to light out and wander the dunes off-trail. The dunes also provide important habitat for wildlife. A variety of birds nest, rest, or winter in the dunes, from tiny snowy plovers and songbirds to swans, ospreys, and bald eagles. Recently, habitat enhancement projects have been undertaken to improve conditions for wildlife in the dunes' wetlands.

Unfortunately, from a hiker's perspective, portions of the dunes are used by ORVs as well. As this book was going to press, however, the Forest Service—which manages the Oregon Dunes NRA—was in the process of developing a new management plan for the area to guide its development for the next ten to fifteen years. Its current "preferred alternative" plan would cut back significantly (though not eliminate) the acreage in which ORVs would be allowed. On the northern part of the dunes, between Florence and Tahkenitch Creek, the new plan proposes cutting back on ORV use around the mouth of the Siltcoos River, where the focus would switch to enhancement of wildlife habitat and viewing opportunities. It also recommends that the Siltcoos River and Tahkenitch Creek be included in the federal Wild and Scenic River System, which will have the effect of limiting development along these rivers and of enhancing their natural features. As a result, by the time this book is available in bookstores, it's likely that many areas formerly dedicated to ORV use will again be quiet, welcoming hikers and bird watchers. New trails may also have been developed in addition to those described herein.

When hiking in the dunes, it's wise to take certain precautions, including taking adequate drinking water. It's easy to become disoriented in foggy weather, and wind and rain can erase footprints pretty quickly. Especially if you're exploring off-trail, pick out obvious landmarks to help you retrace your route. Steer children away from digging tunnels in sand hills; collapse of such a tunnel could have disastrous consequences.

Bird Watching. Certain parts of the north dunes are particularly appealing to bird watchers. One is just east of the third beach parking lot on South Jetty Road; look for a low, grassy levee just south of the parking area perpendicular to the road. A formal wetlands trail and observation area are to be built here in the future. Large flocks of swans may be seen in this area in the winter; various other birds frequent the wetlands here year-round. Other productive wetlands are arranged around the mouth of the Siltcoos. The 0.5-mile Lagoon Trail follows an old arm of the Siltcoos River around Lagoon Campground; if you're very lucky you might see a bittern during nesting season. Waxmyrtle Trail leads toward a large marsh where you have a good chance of seeing wild birds and possibly otters and beavers at work.

Canoeing. There are a number of large freshwater lakes in the dunes, some surrounded by homes and others mostly by forest. Though motorboats are allowed in nearly all the dunes lakes, canoeists may enjoy exploring even the larger lakes' narrow fingers as well. A concession at Cleawox Lake in Jesse Honeyman State Park rents canoes as well as rowboats and the more popular pedal boats in the summertime; there are no motorboats, but it's a busy place on a sunny summer day.

More appealing for canoeing is the Siltcoos River. It's slow-flowing, but watch for snags and be prepared for low-hanging shrubbery. Begin either at the boat launch at Tyee Campground or at a dock on Siltcoos Lake. From the lake's outlet, float downstream, turning around at a dam about thirty minutes' float from the lake. The dam is owned by International Paper, which also owns the land on the south side of the river. You could also portage the dam and continue downstream, timing your return with the incoming tide or

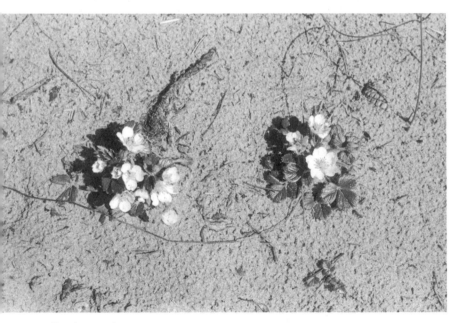

Beach strawberry

taking out near Waxmyrtle Campground (though there is no developed boat launch here).

Beach Access. The quickest car-to-beach access in the north section of the dunes is from one of several beach access parking areas south of the Siuslaw River's south jetty and from the beach access at the end of Siltcoos Beach Road. Another way to reach isolated stretches of beach is to hike there. Waxmyrtle Trail, Carter Dunes and Taylor Dunes trails, and Oregon Dunes Overlook Trail all lead out to the beach.

Hiking. The entire Oregon Dunes NRA offers a wealth of hiking opportunities, particularly in the north. At the mouth of the Siltcoos River, Waxmyrtle and Lagoon trails offer good bird watching; hike one or make a day of it and wander both, plus Chief Tsiltcoos Trail. Inland, the Siltcoos Lake Trail travels through deep forest to a lake also accessible via boat. Carter Dunes Trail and Taylor Dunes Trail offer short hikes to, or through, the dunes, and 0.5 mile of Taylor Dunes Trail is accessible to both disabled and able-bodied visitors. These two trails may be linked to create a 2-mile loop that takes in the beach as well as coastal forest and dunes; this is especially appealing in winter, when there are few hikers about and the campground road (which you must walk on to complete the loop) is closed to cars for the season. For a slightly longer loop hike that includes 1.5 miles of beach walking, consider the Oregon Dunes Overlook Trail. Jesse Honeyman State Park offers access to open sand for trailless exploring as well as some easy paths for families to walk.

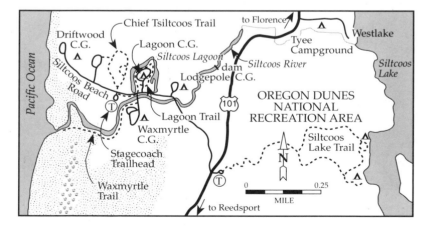

123

Waxmyrtle Trail

1.5 miles

Park in the Stagecoach Trailhead parking area 1 mile west of US 101 on Siltcoos Beach Road, just west of the entrance to Waxmyrtle Campground. Follow the trail 0.1 mile east to the Waxmyrtle Campground road, cross the Siltcoos River, and turn west where the trail begins following the river's south bank. Climb a short hill up a forest of pines and then descend onto the grassy dunes near the river's mouth. Continue about 0.7 mile to the ocean. Or, to do

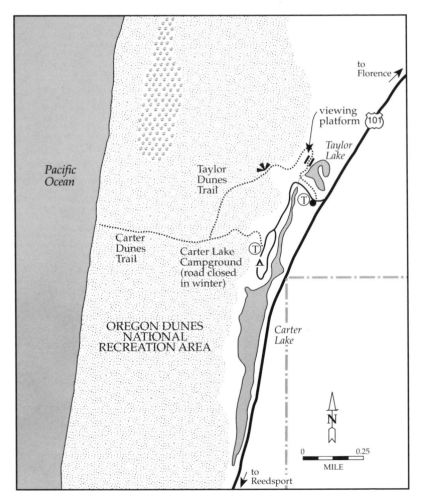

some wildlife watching, follow the river shore for about 100 yards past the forest's edge and then head south into the dunes a short distance. Cross a sand road and continue until you see a marsh. Wild birds use the marsh year-round, as well as beavers and otters.

Lagoon Trail (also known as the River of No Return Loop Trail)

1-mile loop

The trail begins on the north side of the Siltcoos Beach Road directly across from the entrance to Waxmyrtle Campground; park in the Stagecoach Trailhead parking area (see Waxmyrtle Trail, above), and follow the trail, parallel to the road, 0.1 mile east. Cross the beach road on foot and pick up the boardwalk along the lagoon. It turns quickly into a footpath—marshy in spots—following the water's edge. Walk quietly, watching for bitterns, cinnamon teals, and other waterfowl and songbirds. After 0.25 mile the trail temporarily leaves the lagoon's edge but returns, following the lagoon to loop around the campground and back to the road.

Chief Tsiltcoos Trail

1.25-mile loop

Park at the Stagecoach Trailhead, just west of Waxmyrtle Campground on the Siltcoos Beach Road (see Waxmyrtle Trail, above). The trail starts just across the beach road and quickly splits to form the loop. Taking the right fork, follow the trail up into the woods, listening for the many songbirds that inhabit the forest. A 0.1-mile spur to the left loops to the top of the knoll and back to the main trail. Otherwise, continue on the main trail. At about 0.6 mile a spur to the right leads to Driftwood II Campground (primarily for ORV users); to continue the loop, stay on the main trail back to your starting point.

Siltcoos Lake Trail

5-mile loop, 600-foot elevation gain

The trailhead is just across US 101 from the Siltcoos Beach Road, about 7 miles south of Florence. Begin hiking up a steady incline through dense shrubbery. The trail levels off and then splits into two trails at 1 mile. Either direction leads to the lake in a little more than 1 mile. Taking the left-hand trail, the route drops slowly through second-growth forest logged long ago (look for old-time loggers' springboard notches in stumps). At 2.2 miles the trail meets the first group of lakeside campsites. There is one more campsite to the south, as well as an outhouse.

Complete the loop by following the trail around to the south, over trail and boardwalk and up a set of stairs. (A spur trail 0.7 mile from the lake leads south to more campsites.) The trail skirts the bottom of a clearcut 0.3 mile before completing the loop. Bear left to return to the trailhead.

Taylor Dunes Trail
1 mile

The trail begins at a parking area just off US 101, at the entrance to Carter Lake Campground, 8 miles south of Florence (see map, page 124). Cross the campground road and begin walking along Taylor Lake. A boardwalk viewing platform invites hikers to pause at the pond and watch for birds; ospreys are among those that frequent the lake. Continue following the barrier-free trail as it climbs up the hillside at a gradual grade. At 0.5 mile the trail reaches a viewpoint at the edge of the open sand. Turn around here or, to continue to the beach, follow trail posts another 0.5 mile through the dunes to where the trail intersects Carter Dunes Trail heading toward the beach. The intersection may not be well marked; look for a trail marker to the east or, to the west, a foot-

Sandpiper

path entering a shrubby pine grove. To make a 2-mile loop, return to the campground road on Carter Dunes Trail and walk out to your car on the campground road.

Carter Dunes Trail
0.75 mile

The trailhead is 0.4 mile from US 101 on the west side of the road into Carter Lake Campground (see map, page 124), 8 miles south of Florence. (The campground road is closed in winter; park at the Taylor Dunes trailhead and walk the road 0.4 mile to the Carter Dunes trailhead.) Walk 0.1 mile up through dense forest to the edge of the open dunes. Follow blue-topped trail posts across the sand to where the trail resumes at a grove of pines. Continue

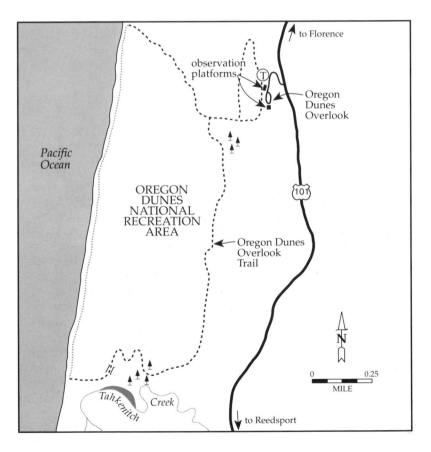

through the trees and follow marker posts across more open sand. Cross the deflation plain on clear (but sometimes soggy) trail; then head up and over the last dune to drop down onto the beach. For a 2-mile loop, link this trail with Taylor Dunes Trail (see above).

Oregon Dunes Overlook Trail
3.3-mile loop, 140-foot elevation loss

The trail starts at the Oregon Dunes Overlook off US 101, about 10 miles south of Florence (and about the same distance north of Reedsport). You can reach the main trail from one of two directions; either walk down a winding, sandy trail from the upper viewing deck, or follow the long switchbacks on the trail leading down the hill from the main covered viewing structure adjacent to the parking lot. Both approaches take you to the middle of an open dune; from here, posts mark the route west across about 0.3 mile of open sand. To reach the beach, bear right with the posts to enter the deflation plain, which the trail crosses with help from small bridges. Climbing over the foredune, the trail reaches the beach at 1 mile.

Dune Landforms

Take a couple of hikes on Oregon's coastal dunes and you'll quickly recognize a particular pattern of landforms. Following are some definitions to help you identify the most easily recognizable elements of the dunes landscape.

Foredune. The big sand seawall directly behind the beach. Though they look natural enough, foredunes are actually a direct result of the introduction of European beach grass around the year 1900. The grass was planted around the mouths of several Oregon rivers to stabilize dunes that threatened to close river channels to boat traffic. Beach grass creates a windbreak, causing wind-borne sand to fall and build up around the base of a plant; as it does, new shoots and roots grow. With this process a foredune can grow as much as twelve inches a year.

Hummocks. The knoblike mounds behind a foredune.

Open sand crossing on Oregon Dunes Overlook Trail

Some are dry, composed primarily of open sand; others are wet, supporting many plant species.

Deflation Plain. The wet, vegetated depression inland from a foredune. As a foredune grows, winds scour lighter-weight sand particles out of the sand bed behind it, effectively deflating it down to the water table.

Tree Islands. The steep-sloped miniforests isolated by shifting sands from the transition forest farther inland. The same varieties of trees and understory plants found in the transition forest are generally found here.

Transition Forest. The approximately mile-wide plant community between the dunes and the coastal forest. Plants common to the transition forest include the Sitka spruce, western hemlock, and Douglas fir, plus rhododendron, evergreen huckleberry, and salmonberry. The most common tree is the shore pine, which is not found in the coastal forest. The density of some plant species creates a virtually impenetrable thicket in places.

To continue on the loop, walk south along the beach for 1.5 miles until you see a trail post (if you reach Tahkenitch Creek, you've gone too far). Follow the trail as it climbs over the foredune, crosses a footbridge, and leads up into a "tree island" of shore pines. From here, posts mark the way across open dunes to another tree island and then back on open sand. Skirt just west of a third tree island (the post, nearly buried in sand, may be a little hard to see). Near the end of the loop, the trail becomes a narrow path through the deflation plain before it rejoins the trail back to the overlook.

Jesse Honeyman State Park

As a dunes base camp for families, Jesse Honeyman State Park can't be beat. It's huge—nearly 400 campsites—with most campsites somewhat buffered by woods. Reservations are accepted for

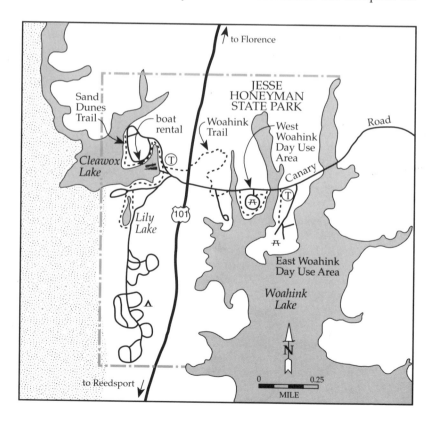

the summer months. The setting is magnificent, with May-blooming rhododendrons towering among the shore pines and Douglas firs.

In summer the water of sand-bottomed Cleawox Lake is relatively warm; you'll find a sandy, roped-off swimming area and swimming platform at one of the park's day-use areas, plus boat rentals (canoes, rowboats, and pedal boats), a snack bar, and a small grocery. The asphalt Sand Dunes Trail winds around the lake's eastern perimeter. At the southwest end of the trail are a picnic area and a second, slightly quieter swimming area by a huge sand dune that descends to the lake—a magnet for kids, who enjoy struggling up and "skiing" back down the sand. Lily Lake lies between the campground and Cleawox Lake; if you're on foot between the two, take the 0.25-mile trail that follows the lake's western shoreline, thereby avoiding walking on the park road along the lake's eastern edge.

A couple of trails lead west from the campground to the open dunes. There are no formal trails across the dunes from Honeyman, but you can explore on your own. The only drawback: the buzzing of ORV engines disturbingly near the park's perimeter, though that may change with a new dunes management plan.

There's also a trail from Cleawox Lake to Woahink Lake, across the highway, allowing you to access the swimming, boating, and picnic facilities at Woahink by foot. Woahink doesn't have boat rentals or a snack bar, but it does have its own roped-off swimming area with a more gradually sloping bottom than that at Cleawox Lake, which makes it attractive to families with young children.

Woahink Trail
0.8 mile

The trail's western end is inside Jesse Honeyman State Park a few steps north of where the main park road off US 101 splits to the north (toward the Cleawox day-use area) and south (toward the campground). Follow the trail a short distance up to US 101 and then cross the highway to where the trail resumes (unmarked) and curves around for 0.4 mile, emerging on the road to Woahink Lake (Canary Road) at a bridge. Cross to the south side of the road and continue east on the trail, which winds in and out of the forest, finally ending at the east Woahink picnic area.

16

Oregon Dunes: Central

Oregon Dunes National Recreation Area

Some of the best hiking opportunities in the Oregon dunes are to be found in the area between Tahkenitch Creek and Threemile Lake. A collection of trails, some well established and others under construction at the time this book went to press, offers travel through deep forest or alongside a sinuous creek, ending at a remote stretch of beach or a hidden lake. Proposed changes in the dunes management plan (see Chapter 15) call for additional development of wildlife-watching sites along Tahkenitch Creek. Camping is available at

Roosevelt elk browsing near Dean Creek

two relatively quiet state park campgrounds—Umpqua Lighthouse and William Tugman—and at a pair of Forest Service campgrounds near Tahkenitch Lake.

A new interpretive center opened on the Reedsport waterfront in the summer of 1993. The Umpqua Discovery Center has an unusual dual focus: the natural and human history of the nearby dunes and lower Umpqua River area, and the history of American exploration and scientific research in Antarctica. The Antarctic theme stems from acquisition of the retired Antarctic research vessel *Hero*, which is moored alongside the center and is open to the public. An admission fee is charged to visit the center and to tour the *Hero*; both are open daily in summer and at least on weekends in winter. Jetboat tours of the placid lower Umpqua are offered by an outfitter headquartered on the boardwalk outside the center.

Wildlife Viewing. There are good bird-watching opportunities wherever there is water here—in the Umpqua River Estuary, for example. Most notable for wildlife watchers, however, is Dean Creek Elk Viewing Area, located 3 miles east of Reedsport on State Highway 38. A frontage road leads off the highway so you can safely stop and watch the large herd of Roosevelt elk that frequents the meadow here. The BLM has also built an open-sided shelter for wildlife watching in any weather; interpretive signs here describe the elk and other animals that inhabit the meadow.

Canoeing. Elbow Lake offers canoeing free from disturbance by motorboats, though it's never far from US 101; you can put in a canoe at a small boat launch at the end of a short gravel road just off US 101. Lake Marie, in Umpqua Lighthouse State Park, is not very intimate, being surrounding by a hiking trail, but would make a pleasant, safe float with children; put in at the beach on the road to the lighthouse. Eel Lake, at Tugman State Park, has a boat launch, though it's popular with motorized craft.

Fishing. Nearly all the dunes' lakes are stocked with rainbow trout, and many have yellow perch and large-mouth bass; some have native cutthroat trout. Tahkenitch Lake is particularly popular with anglers. The larger lakes are better bets in summer, because the water doesn't get as warm as it does in the small lakes. For more specifics, check in at Oregon Dunes NRA headquarters in Reedsport (see Appendix I). Threemile Lake isn't stocked, but it has some big native cutthroats and yellow perch; anglers who pack in inflatable rafts seem to have the best results.

Beach Access. West of Umpqua Lighthouse State Park are three beach access parking areas strung along Ziolkouski Beach; the

Roosevelt Elk

The second-largest members of the deer family in North America, elk are a fixture of Oregon's Coast Range and its lowlands; sightseers stare from roadsides as the huge animals graze or rest, apparently unconcerned, in open pastures. Early settlers killed the native Roosevelt elk rather indiscriminately, and much of their habitat was destroyed. But limits on hunting (imposed beginning in 1904) and transplantation efforts by wildlife officials have allowed the animals to become reestablished along virtually the entire coastline.

Elk were, in fact, one of the main sources of meat for the Lewis and Clark party while it wintered at Fort Clatsop, south of present-day Astoria. Coastal Indians hunted the elk mostly in the fall and winter, when cold weather drew the animals down from the upper reaches of the Coast Range. As observed by Lewis and Clark, Indians sometimes hunted by digging deep pits along elk trails, disguising them with tree boughs and moss to draw in unsuspecting animals. Coastal Salish warriors sometimes wore shirts armored with ironwood or yew slats strapped together and backed by elk hide, and Chinook Indians used elk skin as the centerpiece of a multiday healing ceremony.

With long, dark brown hair encircling their thick necks, contrasting with gray or paler brown bodies, elk are easy to distinguish from deer even from a speeding car. In the forest, they're most active at dawn and dusk, moving almost silently among the trees. Around midday they tend to rest or graze.

The Oregon Department of Fish and Wildlife manages five elk foraging areas comprised of hayfields, clearings, and meadows on the coast and in the Coast Range; the best-known and largest is 1,200-acre Jewell Meadows Wildlife Area, near Jewell in the interior of Clatsop County, on the north coast. Closer to US 101 is 1,040-acre Dean Creek Elk Viewing Area, developed by the Bureau of Land Management on managed pastures just 3 miles east of Reedsport on State Highway 38. You can see animals at either site year-round, though they're most numerous in winter, when the weather is cool, and early and late in the day. During calving season in late spring, female elk tend to seek seclusion in the forest.

southernmost is used by ORV drivers as a staging point for rides east and south, though they're not allowed along the beach itself between the Umpqua River and the staging area. To get there, follow Salmon Harbor Drive from the town of Winchester Bay or follow signs from Umpqua Lighthouse State Park.

Less well known and wilder is the beach access at the end of Sparrow Park Road. It's known mostly to locals and leads to an often deserted, or nearly so, stretch of beach. Where US 101 crests the hill north of Gardiner, at 3.6 miles north of Reedsport, turn west onto Sparrow Park Road (County Road 247). Follow this gravel road 4 miles until it dead-ends a few steps from the beach. (Watch for logging trucks along the way; the road is narrow.)

Hikers can reach even more remote stretches of beach via the Tahkenitch Dunes Trail or the northern Threemile Lake Trail.

Hiking. One of the most appealing loop hikes in the Oregon Dunes National Recreation Area, traversing a combination of forest, dunes, and open beach, may be made by linking the Tahkenitch Dunes Trail and the northern Threemile Lake Trail. Follow Tahkenitch Dunes Trail to the beach and then turn south either along the post-marked trail through the deflation plain or along the open

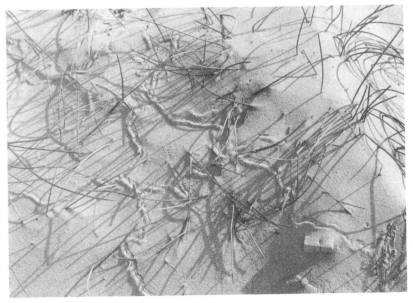

Dunes still-life with European beach grass

beach and continue about 1.5 miles. From the beach, look for a hiker sign in the foredune and follow the trail east 0.5 mile to Three-mile Lake (or, from the inland trail, follow posts to the lake) and return to your starting point on Threemile Lake Trail. The total distance is 6.75 miles via the beach or 6.25 miles via the deflation plain trail.

The Tahkenitch Creek Trail, which was completed in 1994, provides additional loop options.

Threemile Lake is also accessible from the south, via a shorter trail, and the quiet beach at the lake's south end is tempting for overnight camping. But be aware that the trailhead is on a remote road not regularly patrolled, and vandalism is more likely to be a problem here than at more well-used trailheads, particularly on cars left overnight.

Tahkenitch Creek Trail

3 miles

The trailhead is just west of US 101, 1.6 miles south of the Oregon Dunes Overlook and about 8 miles north of Reedsport. The trail drops 0.1 mile to a bend in sinuous Tahkenitch Creek. From here, a footbridge crosses the creek and leads to a loop trail heading south through the dunes on the east side of the creek, providing access to the creek in several spots. At its southern end, the loop trail

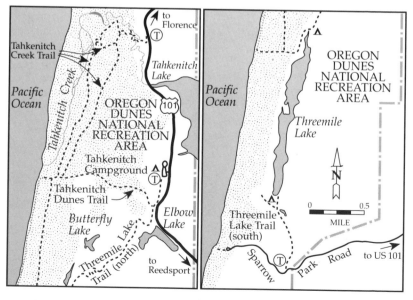

will links up with the Tahkenitch Dunes Trail, granting access to the beach.

Tahkenitch Dunes Trail
1.75 miles, 240-foot elevation gain

The trail begins in Tahkenitch Campground, about 7 miles north of Reedsport just off US 101. From the trailhead parking area, follow the trail 0.25 mile to a junction and bear right. The route takes a fairly level course through the forest until the forest gives way to open dunes at 0.75 mile. Look to the southwest to see posts marking the route. Cross a swath of pines leading to the soggy deflation plain. From here, following posts, pick a route across the marsh to the beach. To make a loop hike, either walk south through the dunes, following posts to the Threemile Lake Trail, or walk south along the beach for 1.5 miles until a hiker sign atop the foredune leads you to Threemile Lake.

Threemile Lake Trail, North
3.25 miles, 400-foot elevation gain

From the trailhead at Tahkenitch Campground (see above), follow the trail uphill 0.25 mile to a junction and bear left. The trail mostly ascends for about 1 mile to a bench with a view of the mouth of Tahkenitch Creek; then it gently descends through deep forest. Listen for the buzz of the rufous hummingbird flitting through the forest. In the early spring, bright yellow skunk cabbage blossoms fill lush creekbeds. Flying squirrels inhabit the shrubby forest understory here, and the creeks are home to eight different species of salamander.

Nearing the lake, the trail crosses a narrow log bridge and then ascends to a rise at the forest's edge, where there's a small campsite. Continue a short distance along the sand, bearing left to see, and drop down to, Threemile Lake. Trail posts mark a route west 0.5 mile to the beach. To pick up Tahkenitch Dunes Trail, hike west on the beach 1.5 miles and look for trail posts near the mouth of Tahkenitch Creek (or follow posts north through the dunes beginning just northwest of Threemile Lake).

Threemile Lake Trail, South
0.75 mile, 160-foot elevation gain

The trail to the south end of Threemile Lake begins on Sparrow Park Road, 3.3 miles west of its junction with US 101 (3.6 miles north of Reedsport); look carefully for a small trailhead sign nailed to a tree at a wide spot in the road just west of a sign indicating the National Forest boundary. (*Note:* Rangers warn against leaving cars overnight at this trailhead, due to the remoteness of the location and the fact that it's not regularly patrolled.) Follow the trail through the forest uphill about 0.25 mile and then gently downhill, glimpsing a pond on the right at about 0.5 mile. Immediately there's a trail junction. A left turn leads 0.2 mile up a trail to the edge of the dunes and down a sand trail to a campsite, where the marked trail ends. Or, back at the junction, you can continue on the main trail down to a log footbridge (slippery when moist) and back up a short distance to a gentle, sandy beach at the south end of the lake.

Umpqua Lighthouse State Park

Umpqua Lighthouse has been in operation at the mouth of the Umpqua River since 1894. Adjacent to the lighthouse is an elevated whale-watching platform from which whales are regularly seen just beyond the jetty and even inside the river's mouth. A short walk inland from the lighthouse is one of the coast's smallest, most intimate state park campgrounds. Between the two is Lake Marie, which has a nice little swimming beach where a canoe could be launched. The lake is encircled by a hiking trail with a spur leading west to open dunes (watch out for ORVs). This trail is a good choice with children, as it's fairly short, level most of the way, and has views of the lake the entire distance.

The park is located off US 101, about 1 mile south of Winchester Bay.

Lake Marie Trail
1-mile loop

Begin walking either from your campsite (access trails from Umpqua Lighthouse State Park Campground connect with the lake trail) or from a trailhead at the east end of the lake, off the lighthouse road. Walking clockwise, the trail begins as a paved path, turning to dirt as it approaches the marshy south end of the lake. It climbs a bit on the west side of the lake, descending again and meeting a spur trail about 0.2 mile before completion of the loop trail. The spur leads 0.1 mile uphill and then drops onto open sand dunes. You can see Ziolkouski Beach across the dunes, but no formal trail leads across the sand and pine groves on this side of the beach access road.

Dunes spur off Lake Marie Trail

William Tugman State Park

About 5 miles south of the turn-off to Umpqua Lighthouse State Park is William M. Tugman State Park, whose *raison d'être* is U-shaped Eel Lake. The 115-site campground is open only in summer and does not accept reservations. You'll also find a swimming beach and a boat ramp used mostly by anglers. There's talk of building a hiking trail all the way around the lake, though it may be years before it's completed.

17

Oregon Dunes: South

Oregon Dunes National Recreation Area

For many years the southern section of the Oregon Dunes National Recreation Area has been dominated by areas open to ORV use, which for practical purposes limits the appeal of any kind of nonmotorized recreation. As a result, there aren't many developed hiking trails.

However, all that may change soon—or may have changed already, by the time you read this—if proposed changes in the Forest Service's new management plan go through (see Chapter 15). The south half of the NRA, from Reedsport to Coos Bay, will be the most profoundly impacted if the proposed changes are put into effect. Dune buggies will still be allowed in a chunk of the dunes east of Ziolkouski Beach (and 1.5 miles south along the shore from the southernmost Ziolkouski Beach parking area), but their use will be restricted in the area of Tenmile Creek. South of Tenmile Creek, ORVs will be allowed in a fairly narrow corridor between the highway and the beach, so Spinreel Campground will continue to be used mainly by ORV drivers, but they won't be allowed along the beach and foredune itself. The new management plan also recommends that Tenmile Creek be proposed for protection as part of the federal Wild and Scenic River System.

The southern tip of the dunes, also known as the North Spit, is administered by the Bureau of Land Management as the Coos Bay Shorelands. There are no formal hiking trails since it's primarily used by ORVs (portions have been fenced off to protect snowy plover nesting sites). The BLM is currently reassessing ORV use in the area and may recommend changes in the future.

Canoeing. Tenmile Creek is a good-size creek for canoeing; put in at the day-use area at Spinreel Campground and paddle upstream to a road bridge, or float downstream as far as you like, but plan to return on an incoming tide. Consider paddling the long, narrow inlets of Tenmile Lake and North Tenmile Lake as well; there's a lot of water-skiing and fishing here, but the more intimate inlets may be quiet. Launch at the county park in Lakeside. Those

Snowy Plovers

From a distance the snowy plover doesn't look much different from any number of small shorebirds you may see flitting along the beach as they follow the advance and retreat of the waves. What sets it apart is the fact that its numbers have declined substantially—enough to have it officially listed as a threatened species in 1993.

Why is this particular shorebird's population declining? Habitat loss is part of the story. The snowy plover nests on flat, open, sandy beaches at the high-tide line around active sand dunes, especially where there are also estuaries or backwater ponds. The introduction of European beach grass to Oregon's dunes in the 1930s stabilized the dunes, blocking movement of the sand forward and thereby diminishing availability of open dunes. Even sandspits at the mouths of creeks and small rivers have been stabilized, leaving less open sand for plovers to nest upon. Residential and industrial development has gobbled up some prime plover habitat as well.

But there's more to the story than habitat loss. Nesting as they do on the open beach, snowy plovers are particularly susceptible to disturbance by humans—and their dogs and ORVs. Any disturbance can cause a nesting plover to flush from the nest, leaving both eggs and chicks (flightless their first four weeks) vulnerable to the family dog as well as to natural predators.

Six of the snowy plover's twenty-eight breeding sites on the Pacific Coast are in Oregon. Only thirty-five breeding snowy plovers were counted in Oregon in 1991. Some forty to seventy of the birds winter on Oregon's coast as well. Among principal breeding and wintering sites are the beaches between Heceta Head and Sutton Creek, between the Umpqua River and Tenmile Creek, along Coos Bay's North Spit, and between Bandon and Floras Lake.

Signs have been posted at several plover breeding sites directing beachgoers away from the area between the driftwood line and the foredune during nesting season (mid-March to mid-September). Keep your dog on a leash if you walk the beach in these areas (or go to another beach).

wishing to kayak in Coos Bay could put in at the BLM boat launch on the Trans-Pacific Parkway, but the bay is wide here and the mouth is close. More appealing to most kayakers would be the bay's South Slough (see Chapter 18).

Beach Access. You can drive to a beach parking area at the end of Horsfall Dune and Beach Road or you can hike to the beach on adventurous Umpqua Dunes Trail. At this writing, those are the only two beach access points on this section of the dunes.

Horseback Riding. Wild Mare Campground, on Horsfall Dune and Beach Road, is designed as a horse camp and, as such, is probably the best staging area for rides in the Oregon Dunes NRA. (The road's name, by the way, doesn't refer to any riding mishap; it commemorates a Dr. William Horsfall, who practiced medicine in this area for more than sixty years beginning in 1892.)

Hiking. There are really only two developed hiking trails on the south half of the Oregon Dunes NRA, though more trails may have been built in this part of the dunes by the time you read this book, thanks to changes in the management plan. One short, pleasant trail is the Bluebill Trail, which circumnavigates a forty-acre "lake" (that's dry most of the year) located on the road to Horsfall Beach. The lake is a peaceful place, especially late in the day when the frogs are croaking. The second trail is the Umpqua Dunes Trail, which is the most adventurous of all the dunes trails, cutting across the widest swath of open dunes in the entire NRA. In fact, most of the route is unmarked even by posts and requires some common-sense orienteering to make it back to the starting point. The elevation figure listed with the hike is just the rise from the parking lot to the edge of the open dunes; you could easily quadruple that figure

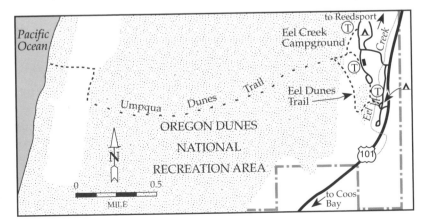

hiking up and down the open dunes. Pick a fair-weather day, preferably a morning before the wind comes up, for this one. The Eel Dunes Trail is mainly an access trail from the south end of the campground to the Umpqua Dunes Trail.

Umpqua Dunes Trail
2 miles, 120-foot elevation gain

The main trailhead is on the south loop of Eel Creek Campground, 8 miles south of Reedsport and 12 miles north of North Bend. Look for a small trailhead parking area across the campground road from the start of the trail. Follow the path through the coastal forest; spur trails lead to viewpoints or link the trail to the campground's north loop. At about 0.25 mile the route breaks out onto open sand dunes. From here to the deflation plain about 1 mile away the trail is unmarked, because the shifting sands would bury any trail posts. To follow the route, head west and slightly south toward the north end of the tree island there. (Look behind you periodically to establish landmarks for your return, since blowing sand may obliterate your tracks; returning, the trail is marked only with a small hiker sign at the edge of the forest.) Once north of the tree island you should be able to see blue-topped wooden posts marking the resumption of the trail and heading north along the edge of the vegetated deflation plain and then across the deflation plain to the beach.

Eel Dunes Trail
0.75 mile, 120-foot elevation gain

The trail starts next to campsite number 50 in Eel Creek Campground (see driving directions for the Umpqua Dunes Trail). It crosses Eel Creek and loops around and up the forested dune to connect with the Umpqua Dunes Trail.

Bluebill Trail
1-mile loop

The trailhead is located just east of the entrance to Bluebill Campground, about 2.5 miles from US 101 on Horsfall Dune and Beach Road (4 miles north of North Bend and just north of long McCullough Bridge across Coos Bay). A couple of minutes down the trail, the route splits at the start of the loop. Heading counterclockwise, the level trail travels through shrubby pine woods at the edge of Bluebill Lake, though you could also walk up the grassy, dry lakebed itself most of the year. At the far end of the lake a multilevel boardwalk zigzags east to connect with the return trail, a rolling path through the forest back to the start of the loop.

Boardwalk at far end of Bluebill Trail loop

18

Coos Bay

*H*ook-shaped *Coos Bay* is best known for the pair of hard-working towns—Coos Bay and North Bend—nestled into the crook of the bay's hook. With all the development along US 101 it's easy to drive along the bay and never get any sense of the wild bay itself. But its wildness is there; you just have to know how to find it.

Coos Bay is actually the second-largest estuary in Oregon, smaller only than the Columbia River's mouth. Much of the salt

Hiking the dikes at South Slough

marsh that used to surround the bay has been destroyed in favor of agricultural or industrial interests, but the bay's many sloughs and inlets still provide important habitat for a variety of plants, fish, birds, and mammals.

Pony Slough, in the main part of Coos Bay, is a central and easily accessible place to do some birding or possibly to launch a kayak. From downtown North Bend take Virginia Avenue west 0.7 mile to Marion Street and turn right, following the paved road 1 mile to where it ends in a large parking area with a boat launch, wind-sheltered picnic tables, and restrooms. In the winter look for egrets and large concentrations of shorebirds here. You're also bound to observe large orange-and-white whirly-birds—Coast Guard helicopters—taking off and landing at the adjacent airport. Time your kayaking around high tide to avoid the huge mud flats.

South Slough National Estuarine Sanctuary

Pony Slough is still smack in the middle of the developed bayfront. For a taste of the bay *au naturel*, visit South Slough, a relatively complete estuarine system and site of the country's first national estuarine sanctuary, designated in 1974. A small visitors' center at the top of the reserve introduces the public to estuarine ecology in displays geared to families; it's open weekdays in winter, daily in summer, and is a popular destination for school field trips. Loop trails lead down to the edge of the salt marsh and out onto old farmers' dikes that are slowly being reclaimed by the tides.

The Estuary Study Trail, also called Hidden Creek Trail, is the centerpiece of the trail system here; it leads through a variety of ecosystems ranging from Douglas fir hillside forest to skunk cabbage bog. Two shorter trails south of the main trail system—Winchester Creek and Wasson Creek—are just as intriguing, however, and well worth combining into a 1.5-mile double loop hike. The boggy ground around the creeks can harbor mosquitoes all summer long; consider carrying repellent. Eventually plans call for extending the trail system into the watershed just north of the visitors' center.

In addition to offering hiking trails, South Slough is a relatively safe, easy, and rewarding place to canoe or kayak. Time your trip to flow with the direction of the tide, preferably launching and landing near high tide to avoid getting mired in mud flats. Launch your boat at Hinch Road Bridge in Winchester Creek at the south end of the main slough's Winchester Arm. For a

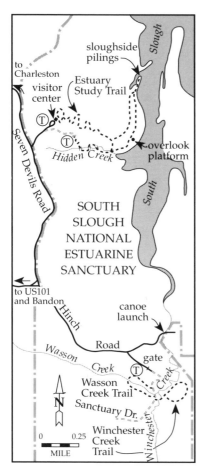

copy of the "South Slough Reserve Canoe Guide" (with valuable route information as well as interpretive tidbits), call the sanctuary at 503-888-5558.

To reach the sanctuary's visitors' center from US 101 in North Bend or Coos Bay, follow signs about 8 miles to Charleston. Turn left at the sign to South Slough and follow Seven Devils Road south 4.3 miles to the signed entrance to the sanctuary, on the left.

Estuary Study Trail

2.5- to 5.3-mile loop, 180- to 320-foot elevation gain

For a 5.3-mile loop, begin hiking at the South Slough visitors' center on the 10-Minute Trail and hike down the hill, following signs to Southside Pilings. For a 2.5-mile loop, begin at the lower trailhead, 0.2 mile below the visitors' center on a gravel spur road. This trail follows alongside Hidden Creek as it drops down to sea level. Below where the two trails meet, a long wooden boardwalk leads through a skunk cabbage bog, odorous and bright yellow in March and April. The route skirts a corner of the salt marsh and then climbs slightly to a large overlook platform in the forest at the edge of the slough.

The next section of trail is called the "tunnel trail" for the dense forest bordering it. The trail passes restrooms 1 mile from the lower trailhead. It passes another overlook point and then heads down steps approaching the water's edge. From here, spur trails lead along the marsh and onto old dikes.

For a loop return, bear right onto the "timber trail" rather than climbing back up the steps. It leads back to the main trail on a combination of footpath and old roadbed; along the way look for tiny sundew, an unusual carnivorous plant species found here.

Wasson Creek Trail
0.75-mile loop

From its junction with the road to the visitors' center, continue south on Seven Devils Road 1 mile and turn left onto Hinch Road. Follow it to a junction, bear right onto Sanctuary Drive, and continue 0.2 mile to where a gate blocks the road at a trailhead parking area. A trail leads around the gate, cutting through a blackberry thicket, and back to the road; follow it down the hill to where Wasson Creek Trail begins across an old boardwalk on the right.

The creek flows quietly alongside the trail, veering away into the meadow around which the trail loops. The trail crosses the creek on another boardwalk and heads up slightly into the Sitka spruce forest. As it drops down to the meadow again, walk quietly and listen for beavers; there are at least a dozen dams arrayed along the creek. The trail ends on Sanctuary Drive, 100 yards beyond where it began.

Winchester Creek Trail
0.5-mile loop

Follow the driving directions for Wasson Creek Trail, above. Walk down Sanctuary Drive, passing the Wasson Creek trailhead. Winchester Creek Trail starts across the road and about 50 yards beyond the end of the Wasson Creek Trail loop.

Begin by crossing Winchester Creek on an old plank bridge. Just past a grove of Sitka spruce (with one massive tree), the loop begins. Walking clockwise, you'll pass an old boathouse used by the Fredrickson family, whose circa-1905 farmhouse can be seen above the creek on the rise. The trail continues in a circle through the open marsh, which is sometimes completely submerged during winter high tides. Little boardwalks carry you over particularly wet spots. Continue to the end of the loop and back out to Sanctuary Drive.

Old pilings and crumbling dike off Estuary Study Trail

Estuaries

Oregon's bays are essentially drowned river mouths, flooded by rising seas after the retreat of the last ice age. The term *bay* usually refers to the landform created at the continent's edge; *estuary* refers to the body of water within the bay, where fresh water running out of coastal rivers and salt water cycled in by the tides mix to create a complex and biologically productive environment supporting a wealth of plant life and creating important habitat for fish and shellfish, birds, and pinnipeds. Compared with Washington and California, Oregon doesn't have very large estuaries, but it has lots of them: twenty-two formally classified estuaries, from the huge Columbia River's mouth to the tiny estuary at the outlet of the Winchuck River.

Hundreds of species depend upon estuaries for all or part of their life cycles. Among them are many full-time residents, such as shrimp, crabs, and other invertebrates. Ocean-dwelling crabs return to estuaries to feed and breed. Among fish species, such ocean fish as herring and anchovies use estuaries to spawn, and young salmon and steelhead migrating down rivers use estuaries as a place to gently acclimate to seawater before their ocean journey. Among the pinnipeds, it's common to see harbor seals bobbing in bays or lounging on bay shores year-round, feeding on anchovies and other fish.

A great variety of birds use estuaries for just a season: shorebirds range the mud flats for a bite to eat in the spring and fall, when ducks bob on the swells or graze the shoreline; pelicans dive for fish in summer. Other birds live by estuaries year-round, from great blue herons at the water's edge to bald eagles soaring high above.

19

Charleston to Bullards Beach

South of Coos Bay, US 101 heads south on an inland route that doesn't reach the shoreline again until Bandon. Drivers following that route would miss one of the most dramatic and interesting sections of the coast. South of Charleston on Cape Arago Highway is a stretch of state parks encompassing a lighthouse-topped island, an idyllic crescent-shaped bay, formal public gardens, extensive tidepools, and wave-sculpted offshore rocks—all strung together

Lighthouse at mouth of Coquille River

by a section of the Oregon Coast Trail. Just south of the parks are two remote beaches with interesting shoreline hiking.

Sunset Bay, Shore Acres, and Cape Arago State Parks

The beach at Sunset Bay State Park is popular in summer, both because of its gradual sandy beach and its relatively warm water, thanks to an enclosed cove. Tidepools form on rock shelves and among boulders at the north and south ends of the crescent; the tidepools to the north are the more extensive and appear to be the safest as well. The park includes a large campground that is located just inland from the beach (reservations accepted in summer); also consider camping at Bastendorff Beach County Park, a short distance to the north.

Visible from points south, Cape Arago Lighthouse is located on an island just north of Sunset Bay that's inaccessible to the public. But the Bureau of Land Management and local Indian tribes may eventually open it to the public if their plans to build an interpretive center at the site by the turn of the century come to fruition.

The botanical gardens at Shore Acres State Park originally were part of the estate of Louis J. Simpson, a lumber baron who had a summer home built here in 1906. Among the botanical garden's plantings are many exotic species; at the far end of the garden is a large lily pond. A short distance beyond the gardens, a link in the Oregon Coast Trail provides access to intimate Simpson Beach. The long growing season here makes a visit interesting any time of year, even in midwinter; at Christmastime the local Friends of Shore Acres group holds an open house and decorates the gardens with strings of tiny lights.

Cape Arago State Park is perhaps best known for its wildlife watching and tidepooling. Immense tidepools on the north side of the cape are accessible via a short trail, as are the tidepools to the south (and others in between). The roadside viewpoint just north of the park's loop at the end of the road is a particularly good place to watch for birds and marine mammals, including harbor seals and two species of sea lions (see Chapter 6), depending on the season; you might even catch a glimpse of the rarely seen northern fur seal, if you know what to look for. Harbor seal pups sometimes show up on the beach during breeding season; to protect them, park officials close Cape Arago's North Cove Trail from March 1 to July 1.

About 0.25 mile offshore is Shell Island, where you can often see (with binoculars) elephant seals. With weights exceeding 1,600 pounds, they're the largest of Oregon's pinnipeds. Oil-rich blubber represents about 40 percent of the animals' weight, making them attractive to whalers, who hunted them nearly to extinction. However, protective measures have enabled the seals to repopulate their original range. No clear patterns of migration have been identified for elephant seals, but they do range north from breeding sites off Mexico and California when they're not engaged in wintertime (primarily December and January) breeding activities.

A link in the Oregon Coast Trail between Sunset Bay and Cape Arago makes a nice day hike here, especially if you can

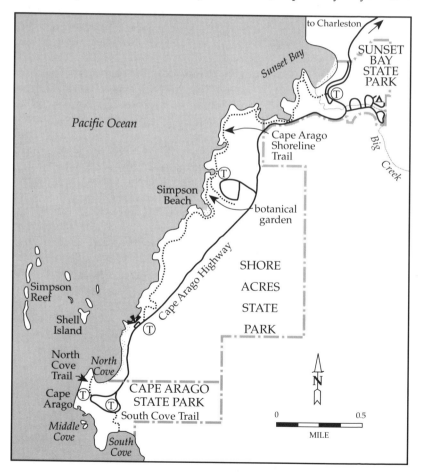

arrange a car shuttle and hike it just one way. It offers glimpses of sculpted sandstone rocks and reefs offshore that aren't visible except by walking the trail. The route is muddy in places; wear boots.

To reach the "bay area" from US 101 at Coos Bay or North Bend, follow signs to Charleston and the state parks about 9 miles, passing through the community of Empire and across the mouth of South Slough. In Charleston, continue south on Cape Arago Highway about 5 miles to Sunset Bay State Park. The road continues about 3 miles, past Shore Acres State Park to end at Cape Arago State Park.

Cape Arago Shoreline Trail
3.5 miles

Look for a trail post near the restrooms at the south end of the Sunset Bay State Park parking area. Cross Big Creek, ascend the headland, and bear right around

Gunnera spikes along edge of pond at Shore Acres botanical gardens

a big mowed meadow; then continue south along the bluff. At 0.6 mile the trail leads back to Cape Arago Highway, follows it south a short distance, and resumes at a stile over the guardrail. It continues through woods some distance from the shoreline and then veers west out to the bluff, granting views of the lighthouse to the north and rocks to the south.

Approaching Shore Acres State Park at about 1.8 miles, you may either detour east and enter the formal gardens (exiting through the open gate at the back of the gardens, where you can pick up the trail again) or follow a trail winding to the west of the gardens. A short distance past the gardens the trail leads down to Simpson Beach, into woods, and then back up onto a bluff. The trail veers out to Cape Arago Highway briefly at 3.3 miles, resumes as trail, and ends unceremoniously at the highway 0.5 mile north of the road's end at Cape Arago State Park.

Cape Arago North Cove Trail
0.2 mile, 120-foot elevation loss

Entering the parking loop at the end of the road to Cape Arago State Park, watch for the trail marker on the north side. It leads past scattered picnic tables and drops down to a large cove with a sandy beach and excellent tidepooling. (The trail is closed from March through June to protect marine mammals.)

Cape Arago South Cove Trail
0.2 mile, 140-foot elevation loss

Park at the far end of the parking loop at Cape Arago State Park and then walk along the road, turning south at the large signboard indicating beach access. The trail winds down to a sandy beach; walk west and north to reach tidepools.

Seven Devils Wayside– Whisky Run Beach

South of Cape Arago is a long stretch of relatively remote beach accessible at Seven Devils Wayside or Whisky Run Beach Access, with Five Mile Point defining the two beaches. "Seven Devils" refers to the rugged, ravine-cut coastline directly north of the wayside; locals came up with the name in the last century. Whisky Run is interesting because of the wind farm on the bluff, where turbines mounted on towers generate electricity from the nearly ceaseless wind here. A

Wind generators atop Five Mile Point

brief gold rush in the 1850s brought miners hungry to glean gold flecks from Whisky Run's black sand beach. A big storm in 1954 apparently washed worthless sand over the gold flecks, though a little gold-panning is still reportedly carried on in Whisky Run Creek.

A link in the Oregon Coast Trail has been built over Five Mile Point; if the tide is low enough, you may be able to scramble around Five Mile Point, allowing you to make a combination trail-beach loop hike of 4.3 miles from Seven Devils Wayside (or 3.1 miles from Whisky Run Beach).

To reach the area from US 101, either follow signs out to Charleston and head south on Seven Devils Road, following signs to the wayside, or turn off US 101 at one of two signed junctions a few miles north of the Coquille River at Bandon. Either route will lead to a four-way junction of Seven Devils Road, W. Humphreys Road, and Whisky Run Road. Follow signs 1 to 2 miles to the beach access point of your choice.

Five Mile Point Trail

0.9 mile, 140-foot elevation gain

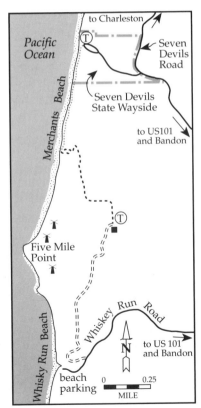

The south trailhead is located at a vandal-marred kiosk with interpretive signs 1 mile up a gravel road from Whisky Run Beach; the north trailhead is located on the beach 0.6 mile south of Seven Devils Wayside (look for a wooden sign in a little draw where a creek seeps into the beach). The trail is a little confusing in places, but most junctions are clearly marked.

From the south trailhead, head north on a dirt jeep road through dense gorse thickets, walking between posts designed to bar motor vehicles. Shortly a trail post guides you to bear left onto a trail. At 0.3 mile, just before hitting a dirt road, turn left at another trail post and follow a fence line, heading west. The trail curves back north, becomes a

157

sandy jeep road, and then narrows to a trail, curving left. Before starting to switchback down to the beach, it passes a bench at a south-facing overlook. To make a loop, walk south on the sand, rounding Five Mile Point, to Whisky Run Beach Access and then follow the gravel road back to where you began.

Bullards Beach State Park

Bullards Beach State Park, just north of the Coquille River, encompasses the 1896 lighthouse at the river's mouth and borders the long, sandy beach that begins at the base of the jagged hills called the Seven Devils, south of Cape Arago. From the park you can walk north on the beach at least 5 miles to Whisky Run, or south 1.5 miles to the lighthouse at the river's mouth. For a 3.5-mile loop, walk the beach from the picnic area to the lighthouse and then return along the sandy river shore. Bird watching over Bandon Marsh can be excellent from the river frontage in the park.

The campground is open year-round; reservations are not accepted. In addition to nearly 200 tent and trailer campsites, the park has a horse camp and 7 miles of equestrian trails. Trails lead from the horse camp to the beach and through the dunes to the lighthouse; another horse trail leads north 1.5 miles to beach access at Cut Creek.

Twenty-four-rayed sea star

Sea Stars

Peek under any big rock at low tide and chances are good that you'll find a sea star—or starfish, a less accurate but more common name. Sea stars are members of a large family that includes sand dollars and sea urchins. Look closely and you'll spot the family resemblance: a radial symmetry that usually divides the circular-shaped animal into five parts.

Most common along the Oregon coast is the hard-textured, 8- to 12-inch common sea star (*Piaster ochraceus*), found in orange, brown, and dark purple. They're commonly seen partly because, like sea anemones and mussels, many live in the midtide zone, which is uncovered by the sea twice every day, regardless of how low the tide is. Like most sea stars, this type has five rays covering an army of tiny tube feet. These tube feet have powerful suckers at their tips, enabling them to cling tightly to rocks or to pry open the barnacles, mussels, limpets, or other shellfish they eat. Once the feet start prying, the sea star's mobile stomach goes into action, sometimes extruding from the star's center to spread itself over its prey or slip into a crack in the prey's shell to begin digesting on the spot.

During low tide, sea stars hang out under ledges and in crevices, digesting their food or waiting for the incoming tide. When the tide comes in, they follow the tide up, grab an armful of mussels, snails, or barnacles, and "dash" back under the tide to eat and avoid drying up.

Several other kinds of sea stars commonly inhabit Oregon's intertidal zone, but you have to wait for an extra-low tide to see them. They include a real whopper—the twenty-four-rayed star, which can grow as big as twenty-four inches across—and a couple of tiny ones, the six-rayed star (up to three and a half inches) and the bright red, slender-rayed blood star (up to four inches). In the spring, the six-rayed star may be found hunched on rocks, rather than sprawled across them. That's because, unlike other species, the female six-rayed star spends as long as forty days brooding her eggs and tending her young until they are able to cling to rocks themselves.

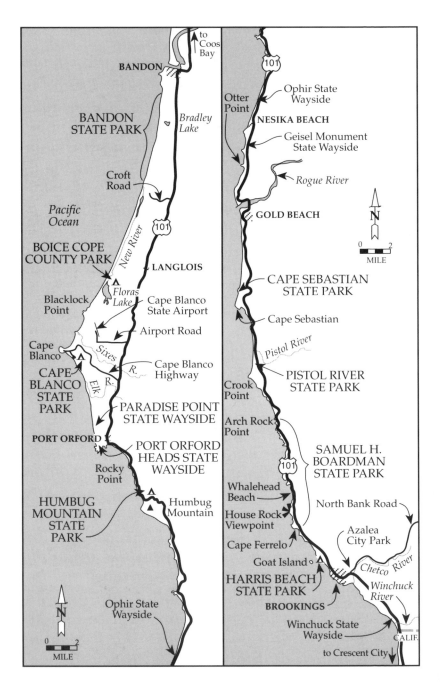

Opposite: *Picnicking near Ophir State Wayside*

The South Coast

20

Bandon to Floras Lake

The Coquille River, which flows into the Pacific at Bandon, naturally defines the northern end of the south coast, falling as it does between the southern end of the Coast Range and the northern reaches of the far more ancient Klamath, or Siskiyou, Mountains. Here US 101 passes cranberry bogs, whose fruit is harvested in October for juice, and emerald fields of grass scattered with browsing sheep. Bandon itself is one of the most interesting towns on the south coast, with art galleries and a boat basin snuggled into its "Old Town." The only youth hostel on the Oregon coast is located here, too; it offers inexpensive lodging as well as an opportunity to meet travelers from around the world.

South of Bandon the beach stretches uninterrupted for more than 15 miles; the south end of this beach is one of the most remote stretches of shoreline on the entire coast. As at Oregon Dunes National Recreation Area, US 101 is some distance inland here. Unlike the northern dunes, however, there are few access trails across to the beach here. It's wild, windy, and beautiful.

In 1983 Bandon Marsh was added to the federal refuge system; the birding is good, with unusual shorebirds frequently appearing between the river's mouth and the marsh upstream, but there's not yet good public access into the refuge. Try getting off US 101 just south of the Coquille River Bridge onto Riverside Road and pull off at a suitable spot along the road. The best birding reportedly is about 0.75 mile north of Bandon's sewage plant off Riverside Road at around high tide. Also try the river's north shore in Bullards Beach State Park.

Just south of the center of Bandon is Coquille Point, an even newer refuge and the only mainland addition to Oregon Islands National Wildlife Refuge. It's located atop a cliff and was acquired to create a good vantage point for the rocks just offshore. From the center of Bandon, follow US 101 up the hill and take 11th Street west to where it ends at a wide gravel parking area across the street from a motel. There is a long stairway down to the beach here, but birding is better from high atop the point. Plans call for development of interpretive signs and a viewing platform here. Walk north through an opening in a white fence and follow unmarked paths

Coquille Point

past the foundation of an old natatorium and out onto the point.

South of Bandon, US 101 veers out of sight of the coast, returning to the shoreline nearly 30 miles south at Port Orford. There are several beach access waysides just south of Bandon, however, off Bandon Beach Loop. Face Rock Wayside has steep stairs leading down the south side of the cliff. Two of three subsequent waysides, all part of Bandon State Park, offer beach access as well. Just south of the south end of Bandon Beach Loop, a road leads west off US 101 to Bradley Lake, a good spot for freshwater swimming.

New River

Farther south is one of the more unusual geographical features of the coast. The New River runs 9 miles north from Floras Lake, parallel to and just inland from the Pacific, before turning to meet the ocean. The Bureau of Land Management has slowly been acquiring river frontage here and has designated it an "Area of Critical Environmental Concern." Wild Chinook salmon run up the river, snowy plovers nest in the dunes each spring, and thousands of Aleutian geese use the river every spring to rest and forage before heading out over the ocean toward nesting sites on the Aleutian Islands, stopping again in November on their southward migration. The BLM plans to manage the area as a wildlife refuge, with attention focused less on recreation and more on protection of wildlife habitat.

A 3-mile trail system is being planned in the area around the old Storm Ranch, where the BLM also intends to build an interpretive center. It's possible to canoe on the New River, but frequently fierce north winds make it difficult most days, and boating can easily disturb resting Aleutian geese, considered the most flighty of the Canada geese, in the spring and fall. The easiest river access for fishing is at the end of the road past Storm Ranch.

To reach Storm Ranch from Langlois, take US 101 north 5 miles and turn west on Croft Road. Drive 1.5 miles and bear right at the split in the road, heading up a (possibly unmarked) gravel road to a collection of old ranch buildings. To reach the river, continue on this road, bearing right where the road splits; a boat landing is at the end of the road.

Boice Cope County Park

Not everyone visiting Floras Lake minds the wind. In fact, the lake has become extremely popular among windsurfers virtually year-round. The winds are high, but it's an enclosed lake with no real waves and no current, making it appealing to beginners just trying their wings. As a campground, Boice Cope County Park isn't much aesthetically, but socially it's a fun spot in summer, when windsurfers congregate in greatest numbers to sail the lake. Windsurfing lessons and gear rental are available from adjacent Floras Lake House Bed and Breakfast. Ask about the possibility of renting a canoe or kayak.

A gated footbridge crosses the New River at the county park's boat launch. For years the public has used the bridge and the dunes to the west for beach access (it's about a 0.5-mile walk to the beach from the lake). There aren't any "no trespassing" signs posted here. However, the dunes are on private land, and technically those crossing to the beach here are trespassing. Over the years representatives of various public agencies have negotiated to acquire the property for public use. At this writing, however, it is still in private hands.

Aleutian Canada Geese

If the sight of waves breaking on the beach excites you after a long drive over the Coast Range from the Willamette Valley, you've had just a taste of what it's like for Aleutian Canada geese when they arrive on the Oregon coast.

Among the various subspecies of Canada goose that can be seen on the Oregon coast, the Aleutian is the rarest of all. With a short neck and a weight of about five pounds, it's among the smallest of the Canada geese as well. Aleutian geese nest on the most remote of the Aleutian Islands in Alaska, virtually in the middle of the north Pacific. To reach their winter home in Oregon and California, they take the quickest possible route, a transoceanic course with no known landfall between the Aleutian Islands and the Oregon coast.

Two distinct groups of Aleutian geese may be seen in Oregon. A small group of about 132 birds from Kiliktagik and Anowik islands in the Semidi Islands winters every year near Pacific City, one reason why a national wildlife refuge was recently established at Nestucca Bay. These birds can be seen feeding in pastures here throughout the winter.

A second, much larger group stops on the rocks off Coquille Point at Bandon and along the New River south of Bandon during migration to and from nesting grounds on Buldir and neighboring islands and their winter range in California's Central Valley. More than 9,000 of the birds pass through the Bandon–New River area every spring and fall. Some stay just a day or a few days, resting and feeding before continuing on their way. But for as many as 3,000 of the birds this area has become a spring staging area before they head out across the ocean to the Aleutian Islands. These birds will spend a week or more resting and eating, building up their reserves to sustain them during their long flight. The Crescent City, California, area is still the primary staging area for these birds, but increasing numbers are now using the Oregon coast. Recently some 900 have used the rocks off Coquille Point, and more than 2,000 have lingered in the New River area to prepare themselves for the spring transoceanic flight. Look for them from March through mid-April and again in November, though they don't linger as long during the fall migration.

21

Cape Blanco to Port Orford

Between Floras Lake and the Elk River is some of the wildest hiking territory on the Oregon coast, with a major headland—Cape Blanco—and a minor, but wild, point—Blacklock Point—to the north, just across the Sixes River. Camp at Cape Blanco State Park and hike the trails there, or take a day hike among the wind and trees at Blacklock Point.

Floras Lake State Park

One local resident characterizes Blacklock Point as "the land of the lost," or "the Land of Oz." Even if you don't get lost, the place has that kind of feel to it—like you might encounter winged monkeys or fighting trees. And, until recently, it *has* been quite easy to get lost here. Officially designated as Floras Lake State Park, Blacklock Point has never been developed, and though it has a network of trails, they wind rather confusingly through a dense mix of shore pine and salal.

Trail signs began going up in 1993, however. While this doesn't guarantee you won't get lost, it makes it a lot easier to stay on track. With help from the accompanying map and some common-sense orienteering, you should be able to find your way out to the point and back without much trouble.

Why do it? Well, one reason is that you're unlikely to encounter another hiker, and the whole area has a mysterious, remote, wild feel. The main trailhead is at Cape Blanco State Airport, but the trail system is accessible from beaches to the north or south as part of the Oregon Coast Trail route; consider a one-day or longer backpacking trip between Floras Lake and Cape Blanco. These trails are open to mountain biking as well as hiking.

Before setting out, however, be aware that most of the trails at Blacklock Point are old roads with some of the biggest potholes in existence; in wet weather they're virtually impassable without high, waterproof rubber boots (unless you don't mind getting very wet and muddy). Rather than fill the holes with gravel, park personnel have cut alternative trails through the brush where potholes are deepest, but eventually these side trails tend to fill with water, too.

Unnamed waterfall off Oregon Coast Trail at Blacklock Point

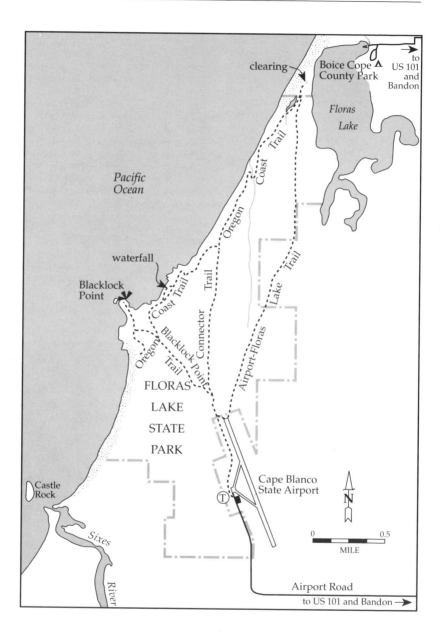

Look at the map, read the individual trail descriptions here, decide how long you want to be out and whether you want a one-way (with shuttle car) or out-and-back hike, and prepare for an adventure.

Blacklock Point Trail

1.75 miles, 100-foot elevation loss

From US 101 north of Cape Blanco State Park, turn west at the sign to Cape Blanco State Airport (across the highway from the high school) and continue 3 miles to the gravel parking area at the end of the road. The trail starts directly across the road.

Follow the main trail as it parallels the runway, offering occasional glimpses of it on the right. Just past a spur leading back to the end of the runway at 0.75 mile, there's a trail junction. Go left. (A right turn leads onto a 1-mile connector trail with the Blacklock–Coast Trail Link.) Continue another 0.5 mile to where the trail meets the Oregon Coast Trail and bear left.

The trail drops a bit and then rises gently, becoming a narrower footpath. Nearing the tip of the point, the dense shore pine forest gives way to an airier Sitka spruce forest. Pass through a clearing in the spruce that's suitable for camping and continue west onto the open, grassy end of the point.

Blacklock Point–Coast Trail Link

3.25 miles, 200-foot elevation gain

This trail is accessible to day hikers from the beach at Floras Lake, the beach north of the Sixes River (crossable by foot in summer with great care), or the

Trailside rhododendron at Blacklock Point

Blacklock Point Trail, which it utilizes for a short stretch. From the beach west of Floras Lake, walk south until you see a little pond just inland from where the beach ends and cliffs begin. The trail starts a bit south and west of where the Airport–Floras Lake Trail starts. It heads up along the edge of the cliffs and then follows a route through the forest, rounding a small cove at about 0.5 miles.

At 1.5 miles, bear right at a trail junction (a left turn leads to Cape Blanco State Airport on the Blacklock Point Connector Trail). Continue south, watching for a spur trail leading west. Take this spur out onto the bluff to where an apparently unnamed creek flows out of the forest and down to the beach in a 120-foot waterfall. Cross the creek and look for an opening in the shrubbery indicating resumption of the trail, which leads back to the main path at about 2 miles. Between here and the Blacklock Point Trail the potholes are as big as they are anywhere on this trail system; take care in winter.

The trail meets Blacklock Point Trail at about 2.5 miles; bear right, hike about 0.25 mile, and then continue straight at a junction (the Blacklock Point Trail bears right). The trail makes a slow loop to the east and south and then switchbacks the final stretch to the beach, ending about 1 mile north of the mouth of the Sixes River.

Gorse

An otherwise mild-mannered wildflower guidebook calls it "a wicked thing," and most residents of the southern Oregon coast would agree. From a distance gorse looks like Scotch broom, with its small green leaves and bright yellow blossoms that bloom from February to July. But get close and you'll see its signature needle-sharp thorns. And broom's invasive habits are rivaled by those of gorse, which is quickly taking over roadsides and other open land on Oregon's south coast.

Gorse (*Ulex europaeus*) is believed to have been brought over from England in the late nineteenth century; it was first noted in a Bandon garden in 1894. In its native England, gorse was used as a hedge to corral livestock. Apparently it isn't a problem in England because of insects that feed on it and keep its spread in check. On the West Coast, however, it has

Blacklock Point Connector Trail

1 mile

This trail follows a fairly level and clearly defined route on an old potholed roadbed. It functions mainly as a shortcut or a link trail to create a loop hike with one of the other trails at Blacklock Point. It is accessed, as the map indicates, from either the Blacklock Point Trail or the Blacklock Point–Coast Trail Link.

Airport–Floras Lake Trail

2.6 miles, 200-foot elevation loss

For driving directions, see Blacklock Point Trail. From Cape Blanco State Airport, follow the signed trail 0.75 mile and turn right on an unmarked spur trail that leads 0.1 mile to the end of the airport runway. Cross the end of the runway and pick up the trail heading north. The trail winds slightly as it descends gradually through the forest, eventually dropping onto a circular dirt clearing and then onto the beach, 2.6 miles from the end of the runway. Continue another 0.4 mile on the beach to a break in the foredune at

crowded out thousands of acres of native vegetation. Once introduced into Coos County, it spread like wildfire—literally. Natural oils in gorse make it extremely flammable in dry weather, and this was a factor in a fire that consumed Bandon in 1936.

For decades the plant's spread was limited mostly to Coos and Curry counties on the south coast. But recent years have seen its range extended north, south, and east, causing state agriculture officials to step up control and eradication efforts. Burning controls its spread, but new plants sprout from the roots. Herbicides can kill gorse, but their drawbacks are well known. Alternatively, agriculture officials have been studying, and even financially supporting, experiments in New Zealand that are attempting to kill or control the spread of gorse with a European spider mite that feeds on the plant's foliage.

Floras Lake. Return as you came, or follow the route of the Oregon Coast Trail back north to make a loop.

Cape Blanco State Park

In contrast to the dense vegetation covering all but the very tip of Blacklock Point, Cape Blanco is bare and windswept. The park occupies much of the nearly 2,000-acre former Hughes family

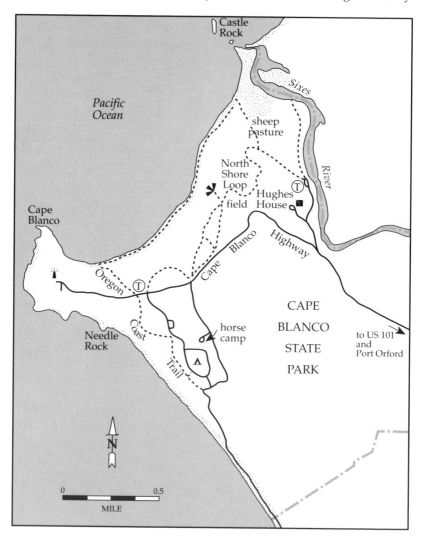

ranch, which began as an 80-acre parcel of land purchased by Irish immigrant Patrick Hughes in 1860. The house he built in about 1898 still stands on a bench above the Sixes River and is being restored by local volunteers; it's open to the public Thursdays through Mondays in the summer.

The Cape Blanco Lighthouse is the oldest operating lighthouse on the Oregon coast. It went into operation in 1870 with a nearly seven-foot-tall Fresnel lens that's still in use and is visible 26 miles at sea. It's not only the westernmost light in the forty-eight contiguous states, but at an elevation of 245 feet it's the highest one in Oregon. Like other Oregon lighthouses, ownership is in the process of being transferred to State Parks, the BLM, or other public recreation agency, which should result in greater accessibility to visitors. At this writing, it is not open to the public.

Cape Blanco is a good place to take horses, thanks to a horse camp separate from the main campground and adjacent to a large, fenced, open riding area. A network of equestrian trails winds throughout the park. The campground is open only in summer; reservations are not accepted.

Recent trail-building activity has enlarged the hiker's repertoire at Cape Blanco as well. An excellent and varied loop hike winds through the park's wild north side; you'll find the tidepools near the cape's tip, a beach with craggy rocks strewn offshore, deep green sheep pastures, and a forested headland. As of this writing, a lack of trail markers makes following parts of the trail a bit difficult (though you can't really get lost here); at any rate, it may be easier to find your way on a clockwise hike, which is how the trail is described here.

For additional hiking ideas (longer or shorter than the North Shore Loop), study the map. You can walk along the Sixes River or to the beach from a trailhead parking area below the Hughes house. Or you can walk the beach south from Cape Blanco to Port Orford, though the last beach access before Port Orford Heads is at Paradise Point State Wayside, a virtually unmarked park that consists simply of a parking area on a terrace above the beach.

Cape Blanco North Shore Loop
3-mile loop, 200-foot elevation gain

Park in the gravel lot near the tip of the cape, where the Oregon Coast Trail crosses the park road (or walk over from the campground on the coast trail). Follow the Oregon Coast Trail north and down the bank 0.25 mile to the beach. Strike out along the beach toward the mouth of the Sixes River, about 1.3 miles from the bottom of the trail.

A mowed trail leads off the foredune and east through a pasture about 0.2 mile south of the Sixes River, but there's no indication of it from the beach (as of this writing); simply drop over the dune before you reach the river and cross the pasture until you either run into the path or you hit a trail marker post beyond a rise in the pasture. At the post, head up the hill in a southwesterly direction, following the mowed path, which then leads steeply into the woods. Immediately look for a trail marker on the right and follow the trail through the forest and up to the edge of a large field. Follow the field around to the right and down another mowed path to an apparent junction; bear left and then left again at another junction just steps away (or turn right for a view over the beach).

Continue about 0.5 mile along a mowed path and into a Sitka spruce grove. Spurs lead off here and there, but you can't really get lost, as the park road is nearby. When the trail meets the road, follow the road back to your car, or take a spur trail through the woods, along the bluff, and back to the road a short distance from the parking area.

Port Orford Heads State Park

The buildings at Port Orford Heads State Park were originally built in 1939 as part of a Coast Guard lifeboat station. It was manned until the 1960s, when more sophisticated search and rescue methods made it obsolete. A short trail lined with native purple iris leads out to a stunning view southward of Humbug Mountain.

Port Orford Heads Trail
0.2 mile

From the town of Port Orford, follow signs to Port Orford Heads State Park and park at the small designated parking area at the top of the head, next to the former Coast Guard barracks. A trail of concrete paving blocks leads gradually downhill to a viewpoint. Return as you came.

22

Humbug Mountain to Nesika Beach

Except where it rounds the back side of towering Humbug Mountain, US 101 offers spectacular views of the ocean and coastline all along this stretch. Trails lead to the top of Humbug Mountain and north to south through the woods east of the highway on links in the Oregon Coast Trail. Nowhere is the beach exactly remote from the highway here, but it's wild and wide, punctuated with dozens of small sea stacks, and makes for lovely beach walking.

From Battle Rock Historic Wayside at the south edge of Port Orford you can walk south on the beach about 2.5 miles until it runs out at the base of Rocky Point. For just poking around on the beach,

Mist-obscured view from Cape Blanco

a little trail leading under the highway at Humbug Mountain State Park grants access to a pocket beach and tidepool area at the base of the 1,750-foot mountain. The longest stretch of open beach on this part of the coast is the 4 miles of open sand between Euchre Creek and Nesika Beach. The highway is close by, but the sound of cars is drowned by the crash of the waves, and on a sunny day the views of the sea stacks offshore make this a spectacular beach walk. The easiest public access is about midway on the beach, at Ophir State Wayside. Southward, the beach ends at the community of Nesika Beach, where an informal trail leads to a loop road off US 101. You could leave a shuttle car here for a one-way hike.

Humbug Mountain State Park

For variety on the south coast, Humbug Mountain State Park isn't to be missed. For the exercise-inclined, a 3-mile hiking trail can be followed to the top of the mountain. At the mountain's base are tidepools and sandy beach, accessible by trail from the state park campground here. Links in the Oregon Coast Trail offer additional hiking opportunities; if you're traveling with a mountain bike, or even a road bike, consider taking a short ride on the north Humbug

Swordfern-lined trail up Humbug Mountain

Coast Trail Link. At the very least, stop for a picnic in the park's shady and wind-sheltered picnic area.

To reach the beach and tidepools at Humbug Mountain, drive into the campground and continue to the western end of Loop C. A road leads almost to the US 101 bridge over Brush Creek; park here and follow the little trail under the bridge and out to the beach. The main tidepool area is on the south side of the creek, easy to wade most of the year. The campground is closed in the winter; to reach the beach then, park at the Humbug Mountain trailhead along the highway and follow the trail that goes under the highway, over Brush Creek, and into the campground. Often the campground gates are open on winter weekdays.

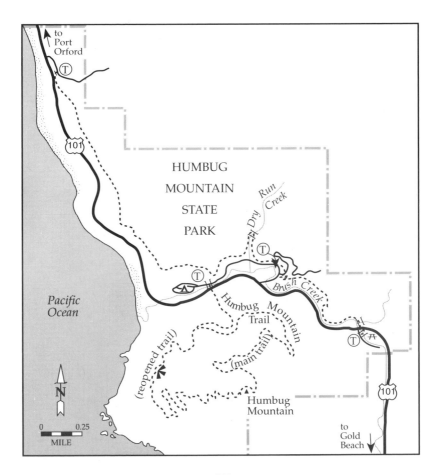

Humbug Mountain Trail
2.5 or 3 miles, 1,750-foot elevation gain

The trailhead for the summit ascent is on the south side of US 101 just west of the entrance to Humbug Mountain State Park Campground, about 6 miles south of Port Orford. (There is also an access trail from the campground that leads across Brush Creek and under the highway.) The trail immediately begins climbing through an airy forest of Douglas fir, rhododendrons, and bay trees, whose

Coastal Weather

Forecast for the Oregon coast? A mild, cloudy, wet winter with periods of storms, followed by a generally cool, dry, and clear summer with some morning fog and afternoon sea breezes.

Temperatures on the coast are mild year-round. The average highs on the north coast are 65 degrees Fahrenheit in summer and 50 degrees in winter; the average lows are 50 degrees in summer and 35 degrees in winter. On the south coast, it's 2 or 3 degrees warmer in summer and winter. At the far southern end of the coast, however, Brookings is known to occasionally exceed 80 degrees when it's barely 60 degrees everywhere else.

Only rarely does it snow on the coast; basically, precipitation comes in the form of rain, from heavy mist to showers to nonstop deluges. Oregon's rainiest spots are in the Coast Range, where even 10 miles inland precipitation is estimated to be as much as 200 inches a year in spots. On the coast itself, 80 to 100 inches a year is normal for the north coast, 60 inches for the Bandon–Coos Bay area, and about 80 inches from Port Orford south. Doused with about 100 inches a year, promontories such as Neahkahnie Mountain north of Tillamook and Cascade Head north of Lincoln City are among the wettest spots on the coast. The good news is that 70 percent of the Oregon coast's rainfall occurs from November through March, and only 10 percent in the summer, from June through September.

fallen leaves crunch aromatically underfoot on a warm day; it continues up at a moderately steep grade. Just past a 1-mile marker the trail splits. Bear left and it's another 2 miles to the summit; bear right and it's 1.5 miles to the same point. (The 1.5-mile route reopened in 1993, twenty-five years after it was closed following a major blow-down of trees during the Northwest's infamous Columbus Day Storm.) At the summit, a small, south-facing clearing grants southward views.

Winds are pretty constant on the coast; only rarely do extended calm periods occur. Even when the sun heats up a summer's day, the wind is usually there to moderate temperatures. In summer the wind is persistent from the northwest or north, blowing lightly early and late in the day and strongest at midday. In winter, the diurnal pattern disappears and winds are influenced by migrating storm systems. Prior to the arrival of a storm, winds are southerly and often quite strong; after a storm passes, west or northwest winds predominate. Hurricane-force winds of 75 miles per hour aren't unusual prior to the arrival of a major storm.

North coast Indians were well acquainted with the kind of impact a sou'wester had on the forest, as the following anecdote from *Nehalem Tillamook Tales* illustrates:

South Wind traveled in the winter. It was always stormy then. He had many different headbands. He would say, "I will put on my headband with which I run on trees. I will travel only on the limbs of trees." That was the time when the limbs broke off the trees. The limbs broke off and fell down when he walked on them. Sometimes he would say, "Now I will wear this headband with which I break off the tree tops." He had still another headband which he wore when he felled whole trees, just as if they had been chopped down. Very rarely he would start out saying, "This time I will wear the headband with which I pull trees up by the roots."

Humbug Mountain Coast Trail Link, North
2.6 miles, 200-foot elevation gain

Most long-distance hikers will start from the north end, but day hikers are more likely to begin at Humbug Mountain State Park Campground, where the coast trail meets the campground road near the registration booth. (The north end of the trail starts on the east side of US 101 just inside the park's northern boundary, about 4 miles south of Port Orford.) The trail is actually a long-abandoned paved road, formerly the route of the coast highway.

About 0.3 mile north of the campground trailhead, the route crosses Dry Run Creek on a wide footbridge and continues along the old roadbed. Vegetation growing on the asphalt can make it slippery when wet. At 2.6 miles the trail reaches a gate; continuing past the gate the road leads a short distance to US 101.

Humbug Mountain Coast Trail Link, South
1.2 miles, 180-foot elevation gain

Heading south from the trailhead near Humbug Mountain State Park Campground's registration booth, the trail quickly crosses a creek, crosses a road, and begins switchbacking up a steep hillside. It tops a ridge at about 0.5 mile, and then begins a gradual descent. Reaching Brush Creek, it follows the creekbank (opposite the highway) until it crosses a side creek on a footbridge and ducks under US 101 to the park's picnic area. To reach the picnic area's parking lot, continue along the trail until it crosses Brush Creek on a footbridge.

23

Otter Point to Pistol River

N*orth and south of the Rogue River* some fair-size stretches of beach offer easy beach walking, and Cape Sebastian offers trail hiking any way you like it: aerobic (up 720 feet in elevation and back down) or simply scenic (one way from the top to a shuttle car at the bottom). The latter seems to be most popular with locals.

South from Nesika Beach, cliffs bar access to the beach for a few miles, but a rough trail at state-owned (but undeveloped) Otter Point gets you back on the beach about 2 miles north of the Rogue River's mouth. South of Geisel Monument (a historic site with picnic tables but no trails or ocean views) about 1 mile, look for a side road leading west off US 101. It's the old coast highway, and it runs south parallel to the current highway. Look closely for an Oregon

Trail winds through ceanothus and salal to Cape Sebastian's summit

Coast Trail post along the roadside marking the start of a steep 0.2-mile trail down the hillside, across a small creek, to the beach. From here you can walk north a short distance to the base of the cliffs at Otter Point, or turn south and amble down the beach to the mouth of the Rogue. Return as you came, or meet a shuttle car on the road leading out to the river's north jetty.

South of the town of Gold Beach, which lies on the Rogue's south bank, there are lots of opportunities to get onto the beach, beginning with the Rogue River's south jetty (follow roads west just south of the bridge) and the unsigned Myers Creek Wayside south of Cape Sebastian, where you can begin an ascent of the cape. There are no significant tidepool areas in this stretch of coastline.

Cape Sebastian State Park

Most of towering Cape Sebastian is contained within a state park whose main features are summit viewpoints to the north and south and a lovely hiking trail down from the summit to the beach on the south side. If you can arrange it, hike the trail one way, meeting your shuttle car a short walk down the beach at the first beach access wayside south of the cape.

Cape Sebastian Trail
2.5 miles, 200-foot elevation gain and 720-foot elevation loss

The trail begins at the south viewpoint at Cape Sebastian State Park, 5 miles south of Gold Beach. Follow the asphalt path west as it drops and then ascends past fragrant ceanothus, heads into a grove of trees, and ends at the tip of the cape. The trail then heads south, switchbacking down the cape through a Sitka spruce forest. At about 1.5 miles it emerges from the forest onto a rock bench above the bedrock at the base of the cape, curving west with the contour of the mountain before ending on the beach. Enjoy this relatively remote beach before heading back up. For a one-way hike, continue south on the beach a scant mile to the Myers Creek Wayside on US 101, 1.7 miles south of the entrance to Cape Sebastian State Park via US 101.

Inland Wilderness Explorations

Upstream from Gold Beach, the Rogue River offers a range of wilderness experiences, from riverside hiking to whitewater kayaking and rafting as well as more passive recreation, such as a jetboat ride into the heart of the wild river's lower canyon. From just west of Grants Pass all the way to Lobster Creek (about 10 miles from the river's mouth), the Rogue is designated a Wild and Scenic River. Long-distance trails follow the river's north bank east and west of the community of Agness, and there are additional trails in the Wild Rogue Wilderness and adjacent parts of Siskiyou National Forest. Several wilderness lodges are located along the river, some

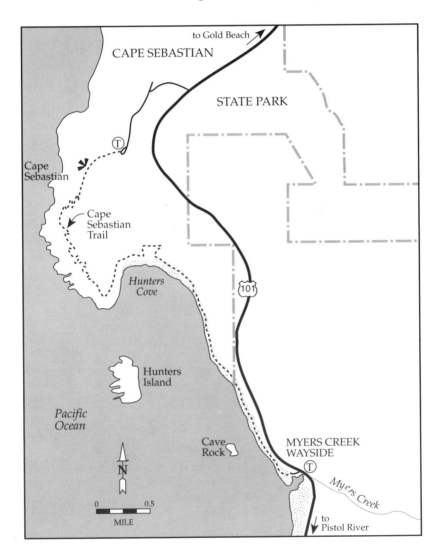

accessible by jetboat but the others accessible only by foot or down-stream-floating raft, kayak, or driftboat (plus small airplane, in some cases). Jetboats are a wonderful way for many people to see the beauty of the wild canyon, though there are river purists (including this author) who would prefer fewer jetboats and more solitude for the hikers, rafters, and kayakers who also enjoy this river.

Just south of Gold Beach a road heads inland up Hunter Creek toward Big Craggies Botanical Area in the Kalmiopsis Wilderness Area. Along the way is Snow Camp Mountain, where a rustic lookout with views of the ocean may be reserved for overnight stays.

For information on exploring the Rogue River or Kalmiopsis Wilderness Area by foot or boat, contact the Siskiyou National Forest headquarters in Grants Pass (503-479-5301) or stop at the ranger station in Gold Beach (see Appendix I). Names of jetboat operators are available from the chamber of commerce in Gold Beach, or simply follow road signs to operators' docks inside the mouth of the river.

Riders pause among rocks near mouth of Pistol River

Sitka Spruce

In many ways Sitka spruce *(Picea sitchensis)* is the definitive Oregon coastal conifer. At Cape Sebastian and other locations it carpets steep seaward cliffs; elsewhere it grows in airy old-growth stands mixed with Douglas fir and hemlock. Its range is the fog belt along the entire northern Pacific coast from Alaska to northern California, where the world's tallest tree—the coast redwood—takes over. It can be found as far as 100 miles up the Columbia River, but south of the Columbia it is found only within 2 or 3 miles of the coast.

Typically, Sitka spruce grow up to 180 feet tall and 8 to 12 feet in diameter; the largest are 400 to 700 years old. The world's tallest Sitka spruce commands a wayside near Seaside, a few miles inland from US 101 on US 26; it measures 16.5 feet in diameter and 216 feet tall at the point where the top has broken off. At Cape Meares State Park near Tillamook, short hikes lead to the unusually Big Spruce and to the Octopus Tree, a large Sitka spruce whose lack of a single central trunk led to its name. Sitka spruce was logged heavily during World War I; its comparatively high strength and resiliency and low weight made it ideal for building airplanes. (It's no coincidence that the largest airplane ever built—Howard Hughes's "Spruce Goose"—was made of Sitka spruce.)

The spruce was important to coastal natives, who wove its long, sinewy roots into baskets, rain hats, and ropes for whaling, used its pitch to caulk whaling canoes, and brewed its inner bark into a tea to soothe sore throats. A story in *Nehalem Tillamook Tales* explains:

Those two Younger Wild Women were angry. They thought, "We have no men who care about us. We will ask everything that is growing, 'How do I look? Do I look well with my face paint?'" They asked all kinds of trees. Many of them said, "You do not look so well. That tattoo does not look pretty." Then Younger Wild Woman would jinx them. One asked Spruce. He said, "You look quite nice, you look real pretty." Then Younger Wild Woman said, "All right. Now, after a while, your limbs will make the best wood. From your roots women will make baskets and become wealthy. You will be the most useful of trees."

24

Samuel H. Boardman State Park

Samuel H. Boardman State Park is a skinny coastline park more than 10 miles long, threaded by US 101 and occupying most of the shoreline between Pistol River and Brookings. It's characterized by an abundance of trails, most of them quite short, leading hikers from numerous highway turnouts to dramatic views of the coastline that aren't visible from a car window. The trails serve hikers of all stripes: long-distance Oregon Coast Trail hikers seeking an alternative to the highway shoulder; day hikers looking for loop or one-way hikes; and highway sightseers interested in short leg-stretching breaks from the car.

Any one of the trails is worth checking out; look at the map here or set out from virtually any of the turnouts in the park.

Indian Sands in Boardman State Park

Among the shorter trails leading to good viewpoints are the loop trail at Arch Rock Point and the Oregon Coast Trail links starting at the Natural Bridges Cove trailhead and the North Island Trail Viewpoint, which leads to a hidden beach. Each of these short trails has been linked to create a continuous Oregon Coast Trail section from Arch Rock Point picnic area south to Lone Ranch Wayside; day hikers can take advantage of these links by extending their outings as well.

The 0.2-mile trail to Indian Sands is particularly worthwhile. Here, alongside open sand dunes, wind and water have carved the ocher sandstone into fantastic shapes; the color of the rock is particularly striking late in the afternoon. Indian Sands is also along the route of the Oregon Coast Trail through Samuel H. Boardman State Park; consider making the 2.5-mile hike from the parking area on the south end of Thomas Creek Bridge to where the coast trail emerges at the top of the Whalehead Beach access road.

The largest day-use area in the park is at Whalehead Beach, where you'll find beach access, restrooms, and picnic tables. An interesting loop hike is possible from Whalehead Beach as well; walk south on the beach about 0.5 mile, take the trail heading steeply up the beach 0.2 mile to Whalehead Trail Viewpoint, and then backtrack very briefly on US 101 and follow the Whalehead park access road back to the beach.

Cape Ferrelo isn't the tallest cape on the coast, but it offers some outstanding views; from the parking area follow the route of the Oregon Coast Trail north a short distance to a spur leading down to a pocket beach (not particularly secluded, but sweet). From Cape Ferrelo you can walk to nearby Lone Ranch Wayside on the Oregon Coast Trail (Lone Ranch Wayside also is accessible by car off US 101). At low tide, scattered rocks form moderately interesting tidepools off the beach at Lone Ranch.

Most of the trails in the park are very short, and trail building continues, so the trail system is constantly evolving. (At this writing, plans were being made to develop trails north of Arch Rock Point.) The short walk to Indian Sands is described below, as well as several Oregon Coast Trail links that take you off US 101 for a good stretch; all are particularly well suited to one-way walking if you have a shuttle car. For longer hikes, see Section 24 of Guide to the Oregon Coast Trail at the back of this book.

Trails here can be overgrown in spring; autumn, when trails are trimmed and weather is often balmy, is a great time to hike. Watch out for occasional patches of poison oak.

North Island Trail Viewpoint–China Creek Beach Trail

0.75 mile, 365-foot elevation loss

Park at North Island Trail Viewpoint, a highway turnout 0.2 mile north of Thomas Creek Bridge. Enter the woods and immediately turn north onto the Oregon Coast Trail. The trail rolls along, fairly level for 0.25 mile, then begins a steep descent alongside China Creek, hitting the wild, hidden beach at 0.75 mile. Return as you came or, if the tide isn't too high, continue north on the beach 0.4 mile to where the Oregon Coast Trail resumes just north of a rocky point. Follow the trail 0.7 mile up to an unmarked turnout on US 101 just north of Spruce Creek.

Indian Sands Trail

0.2 mile

Three generations wade at Whalehead Beach

The trailhead is located at a large parking area on the west side of US 101 just south of milepost 348, about 12 miles north of Brookings. The trail drops quickly through dense coastal forest. Approaching the forest's edge, take either of the spur trails that appear to lead toward the sand, mentally marking your route for your return. The trail ends at the open sand and sandstone cliffs known as Indian Sands. Trail posts to the north and south indicate the route of the Oregon Coast Trail through here.

Thomas Creek Bridge–Whalehead Beach Trail

2.5 miles, 250-foot elevation gain

Begin at the large parking area at the south end of Thomas Creek Bridge, about 0.75 mile north of the Indian Sands trailhead. The trail leads down a draw, into a forest, and across a hillside; then

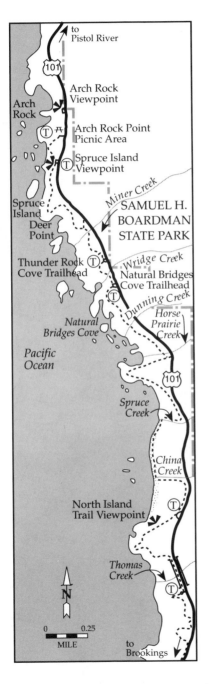

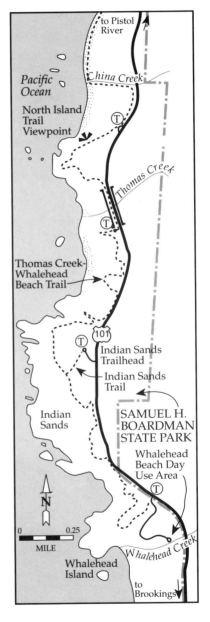

189

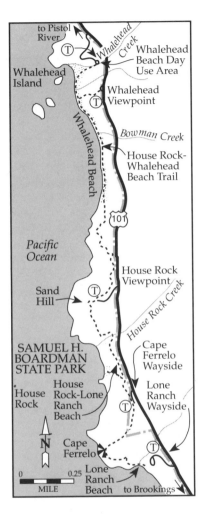

it returns to US 101 after 0.5 mile. Follow the trail just below the highway guardrail a short distance and continue as it heads west to a broad view northward, then descends along the contour of a steep draw, climbs over a saddle, and leads onto the dunes at Indian Sands. Posts indicate the trail's route south through the open sand.

Continue south to where a path resumes. It enters the woods, crosses a couple of creeks, and then leads out to the highway. Walk along the shoulder for about 40 yards and pick up the trail again. It leads into a Sitka spruce forest, climbing a bit to a viewpoint, and drops down to a parking area at the junction of the Whalehead Beach access road and US 101.

House Rock Viewpoint– Whalehead Beach Trail

1.5 miles, 480-foot elevation loss

From the northwest corner of the House Rock Viewpoint parking area (off US 101 between Whalehead Beach and Cape Ferrelo, about 9 miles north of Brookings), look for the Oregon Coast Trail post. The trail begins by descending fairly gently into a dense forest of salal and Sitka spruce. At 0.75 mile it starts switchbacking uphill for 0.25 mile, to a point

Opposite: *Oregon Coast Trail north of Whalehead Beach*

Gray Whales

Of two dozen or so types of cetaceans commonly found in the waters off Oregon, the gray whale is the most visible. Some 15,000 to 20,000 gray whales pass through Oregon waters twice each year from December through May en route between arctic and subtropical waters—at 6,000 miles, the longest migration of any mammal. More recently, an estimated 200 gray whales have begun spending their entire summer and fall off the Oregon coast rather than continuing north. These resident whales tend to stay closer to shore than the migrants and are hence easier to spot.

As for the migrants, the numbers of those heading north in the spring tend to peak around mid-March; cows with their calves start arriving from May through early June. Pregnant females are the first to head south, reaching the Oregon coast in mid-December; the number of migrants builds to a peak of about thirty per hour passing Oregon's coastal headlands in late December and early January.

Calm, overcast mornings offer the best conditions for spotting whales. The most common way to spot a whale is by observing it blow, exhaling water and vapor out its blowhole. Watch also for sounding (exposing the tail flukes as it makes a deep dive), spy-hopping (raising its head partially out of the water), and breaching (surging out of the sea for half to three-quarters of its length, then falling back into the water with a huge splash).

Virtually any promontory along the coast offers a chance to spot a migrating whale; especially good are Neahkahnie Mountain, Cape Meares, Cape Lookout, Boiler Bay Wayside, Depoe Bay seawall, Devil's Churn, Sea Lion Caves, Umpqua Lighthouse, and Cape Ferrelo. Every year for the week between Christmas and New Year's Day, and again during spring vacation week in March, volunteers organized by the Mark O. Hatfield Marine Science Center station themselves at nearly two dozen vantage points along the coast daily from 10:00 A.M. to 1:00 P.M. to help visitors spot migrating whales; look for a "Whale Watching Spoken Here" sign.

within 20 feet of US 101. It plunges down a brushy hillside to end at the south end of Whalehead Beach 1.5 miles from House Rock Viewpoint; Whalehead Beach day-use area is another 1.5 miles to the north via the beach.

House Rock Viewpoint–Cape Ferrelo Trail
1.5 miles, 440-foot elevation loss

From the southwest corner of the House Rock Viewpoint parking area (see above for driving directions), an Oregon Coast Trail post indicates resumption of the trail. It heads south, mostly descending through deep forest, emerging at about 1 mile onto open grassy slopes approaching Cape Ferrelo. At 1.3 miles a spur leads west to a tiny beach. Continue on the main trail to the parking area at Cape Ferrelo.

Cape Ferrelo–Lone Ranch Beach Trail
1 mile, 290-foot elevation loss

From the parking lot at Cape Ferrelo Viewpoint, follow Oregon Coast Trail posts south and west 0.5 mile through the grassy hillside to the tip of the cape. Here the trail turns south and begins descending. Watch carefully for a sharp (possibly unmarked) right turn in the trail; take it and follow the trail to its terminus at the north end of Lone Ranch Beach (or, at the junction, continue straight to loop back to the parking area at Cape Ferrelo). From the end of the trail, it's a short walk along the beach and up the bluff to the Lone Ranch Beach parking area.

25

Harris Beach to the California Border

Known as the "banana belt" of the Oregon Coast, the Brookings area is often several degrees warmer than any other spot on the coast, making its beaches especially appealing for winter beachwalking. Much of the coastline here is inaccessible due to its rocky geography and private land ownership. There are several appealing beach access points, but you have to know where they are—there are few signs from US 101.

Chetco Point is a dramatic rocky peninsula with hidden beaches on either side. To reach it, turn off US 101 on tiny Wharf Street (just south of the traffic light at Center Street, about 0.5 mile

Harris Beach

north of the Chetco River bridge) and follow it west past a fenced housing development, a playing field, and the city water-treatment plant. Park at the road's end and follow an informal path out of the neck of the point. Scramble down one of the trails leading to pocket beaches to the north and south, or continue to the trail's end at a lovely little beach with an excellent view south to the California coast.

Sport Haven County Park lies south of the Chetco River's south jetty; from US 101 follow signs to the boat basin. Surfers frequent the beach's north end. At medium to low tide, beach walkers may walk south at least 0.5 mile, or farther if the tide is low enough to allow you to slip through a small rock archway (but watch the tide for a safe return).

South of town, McVay Beach is accessible via an undeveloped state wayside. About 0.5 mile north of the Winchuck River, turn west on Ocean View Drive and continue 1.1 miles to a grassy field to the west, unmarked but for a sign reading "Park Closed at Dusk." In summer you may drive in on a gravel road; in winter, park along the road and walk past the gate a short distance toward the cliff above the beach, bearing left to find the trail that leads down to the sand. Here there are expansive rocky tidepools and a sandy beach stretching 0.25 mile north and south several miles, past the Winchuck River and into California. Rocky points, some with natural arches and caves, may block progress south except at low tide.

The southernmost beach access north of the border is at Winchuck State Wayside, off US 101 about 0.5 mile north of the state line. The wayside (possibly unsigned) is on the Winchuck River's north bank; park there to explore the riverbank, or walk out to US 101 and cross the highway bridge on foot, following an informal trail west 0.25 mile along the south bank through the shrubby forest and dunes to the beach. If you head south, you'll be walking on a California beach in less than 0.5 mile.

The most developed public beach access north of the Winchuck River is at Harris Beach State Park, located on the northern fringe of Brookings. This park also offers the only public camping in the stretch, though there are a few private RV campgrounds in the vicinity of Brookings along US 101.

Harris Beach State Park

In contrast to the wide, long beaches common to the north coast, Harris Beach consists of a series of private coves defined by

Coastal Bird Refuges

More than 1 million seabirds nest on some 1,400 islands, rocks, and reefs off Oregon's shore. And virtually all of those rocks are under federal protection, off-limits to all but the birds, harbor seals, sea lions, and elephant seals that use the rocks for breeding or resting.

The first national wildlife refuge established on the Oregon coast was at Three Arch Rocks; it was signed into law by President Theodore Roosevelt in 1907. It was then, and still is, the site of Oregon's largest seabird colonies; about 220,000 common murres nest on ledges throughout the rocks, and 2,000 to 4,000 tufted puffins—a "megacolony" by Oregon standards, according to a state wildlife biologist—nest on the easternmost rock.

In 1935 Goat Island, located on the south coast west of present-day Harris Beach State Park, became the first of the 1,400 islands, rocks, and reefs to eventually comprise the Oregon Islands National Wildlife Refuge. Total refuge area is only about 720 acres, but those acres provide key nesting habitat for thirteen species of marine birds. The old-growth forest on the seaward cliffs at Cape Meares became a wildlife refuge in 1938, protecting bald eagles, marbled murrelets, and other coast-dwelling species.

As a rule, the rocks of Oregon Islands and Three Arch Rock refuges are off-limits to humans in order to maintain undisturbed breeding habitat for seabirds and marine mammals. Many bird species are extremely sensitive to disturbance; seabirds will flee the nest at a visitor's approach, accidentally knocking their eggs or nestlings into the sea or leaving them vulnerable to the elements and to predators. For cliff-burrowing birds such as puffins, auklets, and storm petrels, disturbance of mainland nesting sites by humans and predation by mammals on shore make protection of nesting habitat on offshore islands even more important. Refuge managers ask that all watercraft remain at least 500 feet away from the rocks and islands, to protect the birds and mammals there.

The first mainland addition to Oregon Islands was made in 1991. Coquille Point in Bandon was added specifically to provide a vantage point for offshore rocks; plans call for a viewing platform and interpretive signs.

With offshore islands well protected, coastal wetlands have become the main target for coastal bird habitat protection. In 1983 Bandon Marsh was added to the federal refuge system, and wildlife officials plan to establish boardwalk trails and other interpretive facilities here. In 1991, the U.S. Fish and Wildlife Service made the first acquisitions to create refuges at Siletz Bay and Nestucca Bay as well. Pastures at Nestucca Bay constitute the wintering area for the unique and threatened Aleutian goose, a subpopulation of the Canada goose.

Common murres

rocky outcrops, with spirelike sea stacks just offshore. Trails lead onto the beach from three points in Harris Beach State Park: a parking area near the park entrance, the campground, and the picnic area. At low tide the ocean recedes to reveal rocky tidepools all along the beach; the main intertidal area is in the middle, across from the campground. The park's campground accepts reservations in summer.

The park also has a trail leading 0.2 mile to a high point overlooking the coastline. Harris Butte Trail begins on the main park road just past the campground entrance; just inside the campground, look for the trail sign on the north side of the road. It's a quick walk to the viewpoint at the top of the knoll. Looking west you can see Goat Island, 0.5 mile at sea. This was the first of Oregon's offshore islands to be included in Oregon Islands National Wildlife Refuge; puffins, auklets, murres, gulls, guillemots, storm petrels, and cormorants are among the seabirds nesting on the island.

Inland Hiking

Inland from Brookings a short distance are a couple of parks worth a detour. Azalea City Park is particularly appealing in May, when the park's many wild azaleas—some as many as 300 years old—are in bloom, their delicate fragrance perfuming the air. From US 101 at the south end of Brookings, turn east on North Bank Road, then immediately turn up the hill at the sign for the park.

Farther inland, along the Chetco River, is Loeb State Park, where there is quiet camping near the world's northernmost redwood trees. The best way to see the trees is on the Redwood Nature Trail, a loop trail that begins 0.5 mile north of the park across the road from the Chetco River. To get there from Brookings, turn east off US 101 onto North Bank Road and drive 8 miles.

Continuing father inland on North Bank Road leads to other roads that eventually reach trailheads for the Kalmiopsis Wilderness. A short trail (after a long drive) leads to Vulcan Lake; longer trails lead into the wilderness's interior. For more information, check at the Chetco Ranger Station in Brookings (see Appendix I).

Opposite: *Salishan Spit*

Guide to the
Oregon Coast Trail

Steep stairs lead down Yaquina Head to the beach

The Oregon Coast Trail

The Oregon coast offers long-distance hikers a unique opportunity: the chance to hike the entire 362-mile coastline, from the Columbia River to the California border. It's possible thanks to the still-evolving Oregon Coast Trail (OCT), which began as the brainchild of University of Oregon geography professor Sam Dicken in 1972.

It's an opportunity unique to Oregon, for several reasons. About 200 of the trail's projected 400 miles are on sandy beach, requiring no trail construction. Thanks to Oregon's 1967 Beach Bill (and subsequent rulings by the state Supreme Court), all of the state's beaches are public up to the vegetation line. And much of the adjacent shoreline property is owned by the Oregon State Parks and Recreation Department, the U.S. Forest Service, or other public agencies.

As interest in the trail concept caught on, coastal trail building became a top priority for State Parks in the 1970s and 1980s, leading officials to declare the Oregon Coast Trail officially hikeable in 1988. Lack of funding has slowed trail construction in the early 1990s, and there will probably always be some sections of highway hiking, but State Parks officials hope virtually all of the primary link trails will be built by about the year 2005.

It's certainly not a wilderness trail. US 101 hugs the beach closely in some places, and the trail cuts through, or just west of, many coastal towns. In some places long walks along US 101 are required in order to cross river mouths on road bridges. At Gearhart and a few other spots, cars are allowed on the beach, making those stretches a little like roads as well.

But much of the highway hiking can be eliminated by arranging a boat shuttle across river mouths. And there are still long sections that offer plenty of solitude. You could easily find yourself completely alone on much of the beach hike along the dunes between Florence and Coos Bay, or between Bandon and Cape Blanco.

Few people actually hike the entire trail border-to-border; more often it's used for day hiking or for long weekend backpacks. In choosing a section to backpack, think about the kind of experience you want. Lots of beach walking? A mixture of headland hiking and beach walking? Total solitude, or in and out of civilization?

A list of particularly appealing trail stretches (see Suggested Back-packing Trips) precedes the section-by-section descriptions below. Look for practical hiking and camping suggestions in the Introduction to this book.

River and Creek Crossings

Most of the long highway-walking stretches of the Oregon Coast Trail are there just to get you around impassable river mouths. A quicker and more scenic alternative is to pay a boat operator to shuttle you across. You ought to be able to arrange such ferry service at all the major bay mouth crossings: Nehalem, Tillamook, Netarts, Nestucca, Siletz, Newport, Siuslaw, Umpqua, Coos, Coquille, and Rogue. Call the local chamber of commerce for names of boat operators; at the mouth of the Siletz, you'll have to contact marinas located upstream some distance, as there are no boat operators right on the bay.

You'll probably need to find an operator with small boats that can land on sand, rather than larger ocean-going charter boats. Talk with the operator in advance about specifically where and when to meet; often shuttles need to be arranged at high tide to avoid miring the boat on tidal flats. An informal survey of rates in 1993 indicated

Oregon Coast Trail post at bottom of Cape Lookout Beach Trail

that boat operators charged from $5 for a four-person boatload to $7 per person.

Creek and smaller river crossings are another concern. Most can be safely crossed or waded at low tide in summer, when water flows are low. Probably the most dangerous crossings, even in summer, are the Sixes and Elk rivers on either side of Cape Blanco, on the southern coast. You'll probably want to walk barefoot, tying your boots to the top of your pack. Be sure to unbuckle your backpack's waist strap (so that it will come off easily in case you fall), and use a walking stick to help you keep your balance.

Trail Markers

Much of the Oregon Coast Trail is marked with wooden posts, particularly at junctions or where the trail switches from beach to forest trail to highway. Posts also mark routes across open sand dunes where necessary. There is some inconsistency in the accuracy of trail mileages indicated on the posts; some are accurate to a tenth of a mile, while others are off by a mile or more. For that reason, mileages indicated on the posts may conflict with distances in this book (all of which have been field-checked to be as accurate as possible).

When to Go

Summer is clearly the best time to hike the Oregon Coast Trail, and not just because the weather tends to be warmer and drier. Tides are generally lower, making it easier (and safer) to round certain headlands. River levels are lower, too, allowing hikers to wade many stream mouths that at higher water would require an inland detour over a road bridge. September and October often have excellent hiking weather as well.

Though fierce storms regularly blow up from the southwest in the wintertime, summer's prevailing winds are out of the north. For that reason the Oregon Coast Trail route is described from north to south in this book.

Suggested Backpacking Trips

Following are a few varied choices for two- to five-day backpacking trips (assuming approximately 8 miles a day) that don't require much or any highway walking. These are only a few of many possible options for overnight hikes on the coast.

- Columbia River to Cannon Beach. A long beach hike followed by an ascent of Tillamook Head (approximates the route Lewis and Clark took from their winter quarters south of Astoria to an Indian village at the mouth of Ecola Creek).

- Garibaldi to Pacific City. A boat ride to the tip of Bayocean Spit, a hike over three capes with beach stretches, another bay-mouth crossing, and a short road stretch along the way.
- Siuslaw River's south jetty to Threemile Lake (or to Winchester Bay with a boat shuttle). Isolated dunes hiking all the way.
- Umpqua River's south jetty to Charleston. A long stretch of beach walking along the dunes, ending with a shuttle across the mouth of Coos Bay. This stretch will be much more appealing if Forest Service plans to prohibit ORVs south of Ziolkouski Beach are enacted (see Chapter 17).
- Bandon to Cape Blanco. A long beach stretch (including isolated beach west of the New River), and an adventurous trek over Blacklock Point, crossing the Sixes River, to Cape Blanco.

Trail Guide

The route of the Oregon Coast Trail is not always obvious in the field. The following trail guide will help you recognize transitions between beach, trail, and road stretches and should help cut back on backtracking and confusion. The maps function primarily to point out the transition points where the trail changes between footpath, beach hike, and road-shoulder walk. Numbered trail sections correspond with this book's numbered chapters; for more detailed descriptions of named trails, or for more detailed maps, refer to the corresponding chapters earlier in the book.

The trail's route continues to evolve as new trail sections are built or public access to land is acquired; be prepared for the possibility that the trail's route may vary from the description offered here.

North Coast

Section 1

Columbia River to Gearhart

The Oregon Coast Trail begins at the Columbia River's south jetty. Drive to Parking Area C in Fort Stevens State Park near the end of the road to the jetty. Clamber over the boulders down to the beach and head south on the sand. Stay on the beach for the next 16 miles to Gearhart. Overnighters might spend the night at Neacoxie

Campground, a private campground about 10 miles south of the south jetty and 0.4 mile inland on Sunset Beach Road (watch for the road leading off the beach).

About 0.5 mile north of the mouth of the Necanicum River in Gearhart, look for a path leading into the dunes and onto Third Street. Follow it east to the start of the Ridge Path (one block east of Cottage Street). Take this elevated neighborhood path through town to its terminus at F Street. Walk east along F Street, following the main road as it curves (and changes names) until it reaches US 101. The OCT follows the highway into Seaside to get hikers across the Necanicum River.

Section 2
Seaside to Hug Point

Follow US 101 into Seaside and across Neawanna Creek; then veer right onto North Holladay Drive. At 12th Avenue head west, crossing the Necanicum River, to where the road ends at the beach. Walk south on the beach toward Tillamook Head. Nearing the headland and the Lanai Motel, watch for an opportunity to walk up onto Sunset Boulevard, which heads up the hill and ends at the start of the 6-mile hiking trail over the headland to Indian Beach (see Tillamook Head Trail).

Cross the Indian Beach parking lot and follow the sign to the beach. Cross the creek and then bear left at the trail fork, picking up the trail to Ecola Park rather than heading down to the beach (see Ecola Point–Indian Beach Trail). After 1.5 miles of hiking along a bluff above the ocean, the trail ends at the Ecola Point parking area.

Walk up to the main park road, veer right, and follow the road 0.1 mile; then drop down onto an OCT link trail running west of, and parallel to, the road. The OCT rolls along the bluff for about 1 mile between the ocean and the park road, returning to the road at the park boundary. Follow the road out of the park to the main road through Cannon Beach, cross Ecola Creek, and drop back onto the beach at the north end of town. Walk the beach 5.5 miles to Arch Cape; Silver Point, Humbug Point, and Hug Point can all be rounded at low tide in summer.

Section 3
Arch Cape to Manzanita

Heading south on the beach, leave the beach about 100 yards north of the cliffs and Arch Cape Creek, following a little trail that

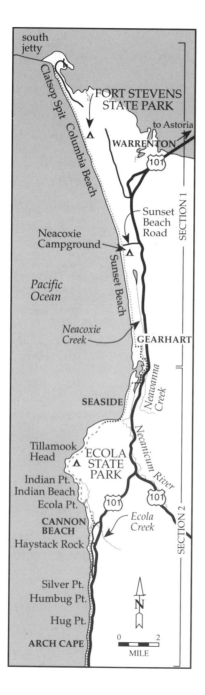

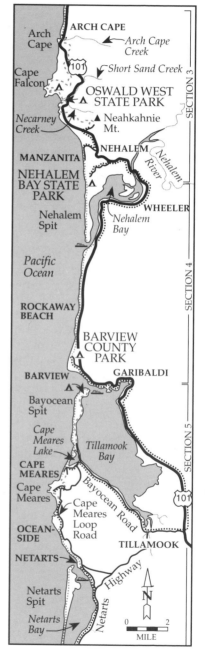

turns into Leach Street. Follow Leach Street east almost to US 101; then turn right on Cannon Street and follow it as it leads south and east, under the highway. Continue east to Third Street and turn right; in one block, the OCT resumes with a little pedestrian suspension bridge crossing Arch Cape Creek.

Follow the trail 13 miles out to Cape Falcon, back to Short Sand Beach, and up and over Neahkahnie Mountain (see Arch Cape to Neahkahnie Mountain Trail and Neahkahnie Mountain Trail). There are a few small clearings near the tip of Cape Falcon that could be used for campsites, but carry in water; the campground at Short Sand Beach offers less solitude but more amenities. At the south end of the Neahkahnie Mountain Trail, walk 0.5 mile down to US 101. Walk south on the road shoulder 1.3 miles, turn west at the sign to Neahkahnie Beach, and walk down the road until you hit the beach and can resume beach walking southward.

Section 4
Nehalem to Tillamook

From the beach at Manzanita, walk south to Nehalem Bay State Park; there's a hiker/biker camp across from the campground's registration booth. If you can arrange a shuttle across the mouth of Nehalem Bay, walk to the end of the spit and round the point; you can see the marina across the narrow bay mouth. (Jetty Fishery, at the south jetty, regularly takes hikers across the bay mouth; call 503-368-5746.) Cross the bay and continue down the beach, past Rockaway Beach, to Barview County Park at Garibaldi (camping available). Lacking a ferry across Nehalem Bay, watch for trails leading off

Crossing Tillamook Head on the Oregon Coast Trail

the beach at Nehalem Bay State Park. Follow road signs out of the campground and down the road 2 miles to US 101, continuing south along the highway. At Jetty Fishery, walk past the marina and out to the south jetty, following the beach to Barview County Park.

Take the park road out to US 101 and walk along the highway shoulder to the boat basin at Garibaldi. With a prearranged shuttle, catch a ride across the mouth of Tillamook Bay to the end of Bayocean Spit. Otherwise, it's a long walk along the highway all the way around Tillamook Bay, through the town of Tillamook, to the community of Cape Meares.

North-Central Coast

Section 5
Bayocean Spit to Cape Lookout

If you shuttle across the bay mouth to the tip of Bayocean Spit, follow the trail north and west to the south jetty and walk south along the ocean beach to the community of Cape Meares. Alternately, follow the trail south along the edge of the bay (see Bayocean Spit Trail) for access to one of several protected campsites scattered along the northernmost 1.25 miles or so of trail. If you take the trail, bear west after the gate 1 mile from the trail's south end, crossing the dunes, and continue south on the beach into the community of Cape Meares.

In Cape Meares you have two choices. At low or medium tide, walk down the beach about 0.5 mile to where the beach ends at cliffs and climb up an opening on the bank to get onto the OCT (marked with a post that's just out of sight from the beach); follow it up to the top of the cape.

Alternately, if the tide is high, or if you're in the mood for forest hiking, take the High Tide Trail. From the main east-west road through the community, turn south onto Fourth Street, turn left on Pacific Avenue, and then turn right on Fifth Street, which ends at a locked gate and an OCT post. (Take care parking a car near this end; there's no designated parking area.) Walk around the gate and take up the footpath heading into the alder woods. The trail climbs gently and then drops back down before climbing slightly to hit a trail junction at 0.9 mile. The beach is a short walk to the right; the top of the cape is 0.8 mile to the left (see Cape Meares Beach Trail).

At the top of the cape, the trail emerges at the entrance to

Netarts Bay from grassy Netarts Spit

Cape Meares State Park. Here, an OCT marker post may still direct you to continue on the trail, but that section of the coast trail is now closed past the Giant Spruce; instead, take Lighthouse Road 0.5 mile to its end and then pick up the OCT leading south past the Octopus Tree and out to the road (see Octopus Tree Trail). Follow the road south down to the community of Oceanside, where the route returns to the beach.

At Netarts, either get a boat shuttle across the bay mouth and hike down Netarts Spit to the picnic area at Cape Lookout State Park, or walk around the bay to the picnic area. There is a hiker/biker camp at the south end of the state park campground. Continuing, pick up the trail to the top of the cape (see Cape Lookout Campground Trail) and descend by trail to the beach (see Cape Lookout Beach Trail).

Section 6

Sand Lake to Neskowin

From the foot of Cape Lookout, follow the beach south to the mouth of Sand Lake. At low tide in summer you should be able to wade the lake's outlet. If not, leave the beach at the ORV access trail at Sand Lake Campground, 0.6 mile north of the lake's mouth, and walk out Galloway Road; then go south on Sandlake Road to the community of Tierra del Mar, where you can return to the beach.

Heading south on the beach, climb up and over the gradual sand slope at the neck of Cape Kiwanda. If you can arrange a shuttle across the mouth of the Nestucca River (inquire with charter boat outfits in Pacific City), continue down the beach to the end of Nestucca Spit, ferry across the river, and continue walking south on the beach. If not, leave the beach at the county dory parking lot north of Pacific City, follow Cape Drive through town, and continue south on US 101; at Winema Road, turn west and walk 0.5 mile to a beach access alongside a church camp. Walk south on the beach until you reach Proposal Rock at Neskowin. Leave the beach just south of where a cyclone fence cuts across the dunes and follow a short pedestrian route over a gravel road and an asphalt path to Hawk Creek and out to Neskowin Beach Wayside. Head south on US 101.

Section 7

Cascade Head

From Neskowin, walk south about 2 miles along US 101 and turn right at the trailhead sign. Here a 6-mile OCT link leads through old- and second-growth forest up and over Cascade Head, rejoining US 101 at its junction with Three Rocks Road (see Cascade Head Oregon Coast Trail). At the trail's south end, resume walking along the highway shoulder.

Section 8

Lincoln City to Gleneden Beach

Arriving at the north end of Lincoln City on US 101, head west toward the Shilo Inn, on North 39th Street, and return to the beach, continuing south to the mouth of Siletz Bay. Hiker/biker camping is available at Devil's Lake State Park; leave the beach just north of the D River and follow signs north on US 101 a short distance.

To arrange a shuttle across the mouth of Siletz Bay you'll have

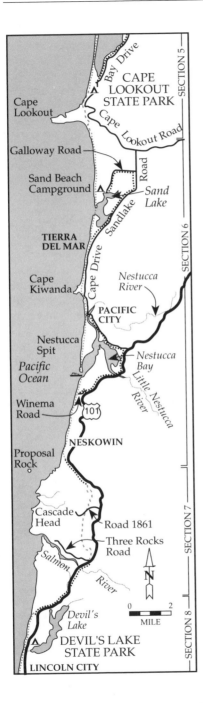

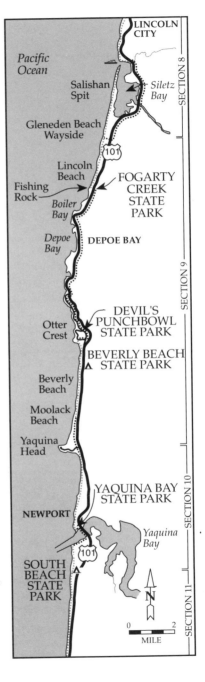

to find a boat operator upstream on the Siletz, as there are none on the bay itself. If you do, just ferry across the bay mouth and resume hiking down Salishan Spit, past the summer homes at Salishan and the community of Gleneden Beach. Without a shuttle, follow the beach south and east along the edge of Siletz Bay until you see a little gazebo at Siletz Bay Park, at the north end of the US 101 bridge over Schooner Creek. Walk south around the bay on the highway and return to the beach at Gleneden Beach Wayside.

Section 9
Lincoln Beach to Moolack Beach

From Gleneden Beach Wayside, follow the beach south to the cliffs at Fishing Rock, just beyond the community of Lincoln Beach. Scramble trails lead to the top of the rock and east to the end of Fishing Rock Street; follow this street a short distance to where it meets US 101 just north of the northern entrance to Fogarty Creek State Park. From here the trail's route follows US 101 all the way through Depoe Bay, since there are only scattered pocket beaches to the west on this stretch.

Tidepools at Otter Crest

Past Depoe Bay, take the Otter Rock Loop to get off the main highway and follow signs to Devil's Punchbowl. A block inland from the Devil's Punchbowl viewpoint, steep stairs lead down the south side of the cliffs onto the beach. Follow the beach south, past Beverly Beach State Park (where there is a hiker/biker camp).

About 1.5 miles north of Yaquina Head, look for a scramble trail leading up the beach just north of Moolack Shores Motel and continue south on US 101. (If you don't mind risking a backtrack, proceed down the beach to the foot of Yaquina Head; construction of a trail up the north side of Yaquina Head from Moolack Beach has been proposed and could possibly be completed sometime in 1994.)

Central Coast

Section 10
Yaquina Head and Yaquina Bay

Follow US 101 (or a trail up the headland's north flank, if it's been constructed) over Yaquina Head. Just south of where Lighthouse Road meets US 101 there's a beach access parking area and, at its south end, Lucky Gap Trail, which leads a short distance down to the sand. Take this trail and continue walking south along the beach past the north end of Newport. If you have prearranged a shuttle across the mouth of the bay, continue to your boat pickup and ferry across. Otherwise, approaching the north jetty on foot, look east to spot the bottom few steps of a concrete stairway leading up a shore pine–covered hillside. They lead up to Yaquina Bay State Park. From the park, follow US 101 over the Yaquina Bay Bridge.

At the end of the bridge, walk a short distance and turn right at the sign to the Oregon Coast Aquarium. Turn left onto Southwest 26th Street, which leads out to the south jetty. Alternately, look for the signed South Jetty Trail heading south through the dunes inland a short distance from the beach (see below).

Section 11
South Beach to Alsea Bay

Continue south on either the South Jetty Trail or the beach. South Beach State Park, which has a hiker/biker camp, lies over the dunes about 1 mile south of the jetty. (The South Jetty Trail ends at the park's day-use area; return to the beach here.)

Continue south on the beach another 8 miles. It's possible to

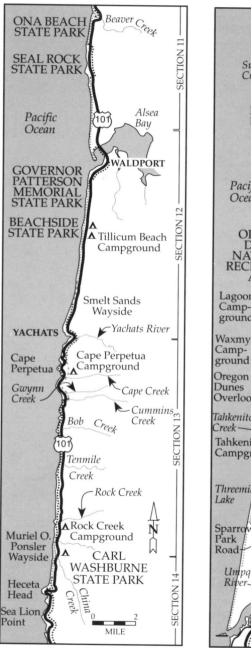

ford Beaver Creek in the summer; otherwise, when you reach the creek, walk across the dunes and up onto US 101, continuing a short distance to the entrance to Ona Beach State Park. Follow the asphalt path through the park, over a footbridge, and back onto the beach. At Seal Rock, scramble up the steep sandstone cliff and follow the asphalt path out to US 101. Head south along the highway for about 1 mile, turn west on Quail Street, and follow it to the beach, continuing south.

Approaching Waldport, follow the beach around into the mouth of Alsea Bay. Leave the beach at the Bayshore Beach Club and follow the main road back up to US 101 and across the bridge.

Section 12
Waldport to Yachats

Follow the highway through Waldport, returning to the beach at Governor Patterson State Park, 1 mile south of the Alsea Bay Bridge. Continue south on the beach for 6 miles, passing Beachside State Park, where there's a hiker/biker camp. You can also camp or get fresh water at the Forest Service campground at Tillicum Beach. Approaching Yachats, the beach ends at a headland topped with houses; look for a little trail running up the sandstone slope (see Yachats 804 Trail) and follow it to Smelt Sands Wayside. From here, follow the road out to US 101 and head south into Yachats.

Section 13
Cape Perpetua to Big Creek

From Yachats, walk alongside US 101 for 2.5 miles to the entrance road to the Cape Perpetua Visitors' Center. (An OCT link up the north side of Cape Perpetua is planned for eventual construction; it will leave US 101 about 1.5 miles south of Yachats and head up to the summit of Cape Perpetua. From here, hikers will continue down the cape on Saint Perpetua Trail.) Camping is available just north of the visitors' center at Cape Perpetua Campground. The OCT resumes at the visitor center (or partway up the access road, if you're hiking along the highway). Follow it 1.3 miles south through forest parallel to the highway. The route follows an old stage road to its end at the gravel road just north of Cummins Creek. Walk west down the gravel road 0.1 mile to US 101 and then begin walking south along the highway, as there's not much sandy beach, or good beach access, for the next 7 miles or so. To camp, consider

Devil's Elbow below Heceta Head

Lanham Bike Camp, on the south side of Rock Creek, or the hiker/biker camp at Carl Washburne State Park, not quite 2 miles to the south. Where the beach widens at Big Creek or at Muriel O. Ponsler Wayside, walk down to the sand and follow the beach south.

Section 14
Heceta Head to Florence

Walking south on the beach toward Heceta Head, about 1.75 miles south of China Creek, watch for an OCT trail post in the brush and follow the Hobbit Trail 0.25 mile back up to US 101 (see Hobbit Trail). Hike along the highway over Heceta Head. About a mile after the road drops back to near sea level, turn right on Baker Beach Road and follow it 0.5 mile until it ends at the dunes. A network of trails leads about 0.5 mile through the brushy dunes to the beach (the main trail, marked with posts, is well trampled by horses). Follow the beach south for 5 miles, wading Sutton Creek. Camping is available at Sutton and Alder Dune campgrounds; for access, see Sutton Trail System. At the north jetty of the Siuslaw River, walk along North Jetty Road (camping is available at Harbor Vista County Park) to Rhododendron Drive, turn south, and follow it into Florence, continuing south on US 101 to cross the Siuslaw River. Alternately, you may be able to arrange a ferry across the river at the marina on Rhododendron Drive, saving a long walk into town.

South-Central Coast

Section 15
Oregon Dunes: North

If you're traveling on foot through Florence, walk south on US 101 across the Siuslaw River Bridge and continue along the highway until you reach South Jetty Road; take this road west and get back onto the beach at the first beach parking area. If you've ferried across the river's mouth, start walking south along the beach. The beach extends uninterrupted for a little more than 22 miles from the Siuslaw to the Umpqua, with a few river and creek mouth crossings that can be waded in summer. Trails across the dunes provide access to US 101 in several spots, if necessary. Drinking water is available at Waxmyrtle Campground (0.75 mile inland), Carter Lake Campground (0.75 mile inland), and Oregon Dunes Overlook (1 mile inland).

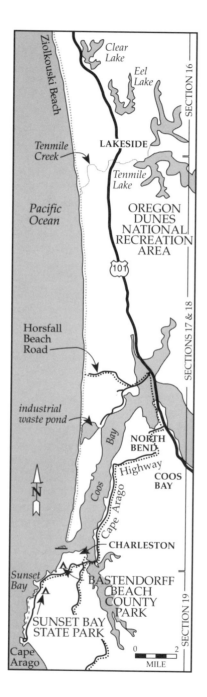

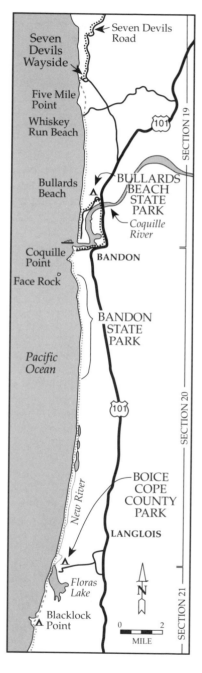

Section 16

Oregon Dunes: Central

Continue walking south along the dunes. Water is available at Tahkenitch Campground (1.75 miles inland), or treat the water from Threemile Lake (0.5 mile inland).

Approaching the Umpqua River, either continue on foot south to the north jetty for a prearranged ferry across the river, or turn inland 4.5 miles north of the jetty where you see a wide trail leading off the beach to the end of gravel Sparrow Park Road. Follow this road 4 miles to US 101 and follow the highway south through Gardiner, through Reedsport, and on to Winchester Bay.

Whether a boat operator has ferried you across to Winchester Bay or you've arrived on foot via US 101, follow Salmon Harbor Drive west and south as it curves through Windy Cove Park until you see a collection of high-mounted navigational markers. Head west into the dunes along the south side of the south jetty to the Coast Guard lookout at the beach and then turn south. Or continue along the road another 0.5 mile to the first Ziolkouski Beach parking area and resume walking south along the beach.

Sections 17 and 18

Oregon Dunes: South and Coos Bay

Follow the beach all the way to Horsfall Beach Access, identifiable by footprints on the foredune. A sand road also leads up and over the dunes and to the parking area in a short distance. With a boat shuttle across the mouth of Coos Bay to Charleston, you could hike another 7 miles along the dunes. (This part of the dunes may be open to ORVs and may be noisy, but not as noisy as US 101.) Otherwise, walk out Horsfall Beach Access Road to US 101 and then south into North Bend; follow signs west and south to "state parks" and Charleston.

Section 19

Charleston to Bullards Beach

From Charleston, the official OCT route sends hikers out to Cape Arago. However, until plans to acquire land south of Cape Arago and construct an OCT link with the beach near Seven Devils Wayside come to fruition, hikers must turn around at Cape Arago State Park and return to Charleston, then follow Seven Devils Road southward nearly to US 101. This is currently the longest section of

New River near old Storm Ranch

road walking (without a boat shuttle option) on the coast trail—about 13.5 miles from Charleston to Seven Devils Wayside, not including the 4.5 miles from Charleston to Sunset Bay State Park. There are no formal camping facilities along the way.

To hike the Cape Arago shoreline, walk along Cape Arago Highway to Sunset Bay State Park, where there's a hiker/biker camp. (Camping is also available along the road to Sunset Bay at Bastendorff Beach County Park, 2 miles from Charleston.) The trail resumes at the south end of the Sunset Bay parking area, near the restrooms; look for a trail post. Follow the trail south nearly to Cape Arago State Park (see Cape Arago Shoreline Trail). Continue another 0.5 mile into the park itself, if you wish. Then turn around and head back to Charleston by road or trail.

Follow Seven Devils Road south about 13.5 miles (the last one-third or so is on gravel road) and head west where the sign indicates Seven Devils Wayside. Walk south on the beach 0.6 mile to where an OCT link leads up and over Five Mile Point to Whisky Run Beach (see Five Mile Point Trail). Continue walking south about 5 miles on the beach. About 1.5 miles north of the Coquille River, look for footsteps in the sand leading up over the dune at Bullards Beach State Park (hiker/biker camping available); follow the park road out to US 101 and walk along the highway into Bandon. Alternately, if you can arrange a boat shuttle across the Coquille River mouth to the Bandon boat basin, don't leave the beach at the state park but continue another 1.5 miles to the lighthouse at the north jetty, or wherever the boat operator has instructed you to meet him or her.

South Coast

Section 20
Bandon to Floras Lake

From the boat basin in Bandon's "Old Town," follow First Street Southwest around the bay as it turns into Jetty Road and leads you to the south jetty. Walk south on the beach from here. (Inexpensive overnight accommodations are available in Old Town at the Sea Star International Hostel on Second Street.)

The beach continues south, uninterrupted by headlands for more than 15 miles, to the cliffs at Blacklock Point, south of Floras Lake. The New River can be forded at low tide in summer.

Section 21
Cape Blanco to Port Orford

From the beach adjacent to the New River, continue south past Floras Lake. (Camping is available at Boice Cope County Park, though at present access is across private land at the north end of the lake.) As dunes begin to give way to sandstone cliffs, look for a little pond to your left, and pick up the coast trail as it winds up the hillside at the far end of the pond. Follow the trail over Blacklock Point and back onto the beach (see Blacklock Point–Coast Trail Link). The Sixes River, about a mile to the south, can be waded at low tide in summer, though it's a large river and hikers should ford with care.

Continue south on the beach toward Cape Blanco. Nearing the rocky tip, look for where the trail heads up the hillside. At the top of the cape, walk east 0.1 mile to where the trail resumes across the road. It follows a mowed path and then leads into the forest. A spur trail leads to the campground (which has a hiker/biker camp); the main trail continues another 0.25 mile until it reaches the park's north beach access road. Walk down the road 0.25 mile to the beach. From here, follow the beach south about 5.5 miles, taking care in fording Elk Creek at low tide in summer. About 1.5 miles north of the bluffs at Port Orford Heads, leave the beach at Paradise Point State Wayside, where a little trail leads off the beach and up to a gravel parking area on a flat. Follow the road out to US 101 and walk south along the highway as it curves through Port Orford. At the southern outskirts of town, return to the beach at Battle Rock Historic Wayside.

Section 22
Humbug Mountain to Nesika Beach

Head south on the beach from Port Orford. About 0.1 mile before the beach runs out at Rocky Point, look for the suggestion of a dirt trail leading up the hill off the beach. This trail turns into a narrow dirt road leading to US 101 in 0.1 mile. Continue south along US 101 and turn east on a road that takes off just past the entrance sign for Humbug Mountain State Park. Follow the road as it curves around to the right, bear right at the split in the road, walk through the gate, and follow the old road 2.6 miles to the park's campground (see Humbug Mountain Coast Trail Link, North). There's a hiker/biker camp near the registration booth. Continue south on the trail to the park's picnic area (see Humbug Mountain Coast Trail Link, South), making a sharp left turn after walking under US 101 and climbing up the bank to reach US 101.

Follow the highway south to Euchre Creek, where you can cross the dunes and get back onto the beach. At the community of Nesika Beach, follow a scramble trail up to Nesika Beach Road and follow that road south to where it meets US 101.

Section 23
Otter Point to Pistol River

At the end of Nesika Beach Road, cross US 101 and immediately turn south on the old coast highway, which runs parallel to,

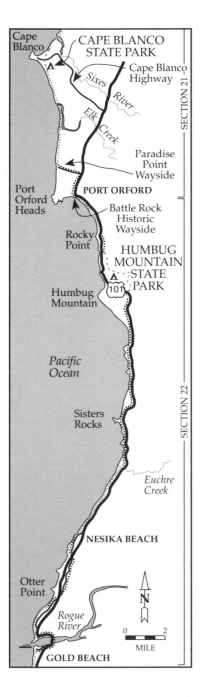

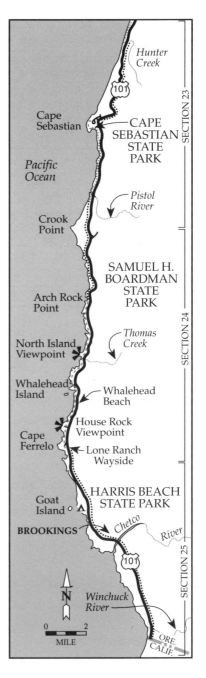

and just east of, the current highway. Keep on the old road as it crosses US 101 and continues heading south between the highway and the shore. Watch for a small OCT post on the west side of the highway; this is Otter Point, though there may be no signs besides the trail post. An unimproved trail rambles down the hillside 0.2 mile to the beach. Follow the beach south to the Rogue River's north jetty at Gold Beach. You can ferry across the river's mouth, but the walk across the US 101 bridge isn't much of a detour. Across the bridge, take the first right, onto Harbor Way, and then turn right again on South Jetty Road and follow it out past an RV park to where the beach starts south of the south jetty.

When you reach the big rock at the mouth of Hunter Creek, about 1 mile south of Gold Beach, return to US 101 and follow the highway as it climbs the north side of Cape Sebastian. Follow signs to the south viewpoint at Cape Sebastian State Park and then follow the Cape Sebastian Trail down the headland's south side to the beach (see Cape Sebastian Trail). Walk south on the beach toward the Pistol River (with US 101 in sight most of the way). In summer the Pistol River can be forded at low tide, and hikers can return to US 101 after crossing the river. Otherwise, cross the dunes and climb up onto the highway where it crosses the river north of its mouth. Continue along US 101 to Samuel H. Boardman State Park.

Section 24
Samuel H. Boardman State Park

State Parks is continuing to expand the Oregon Coast Trail within Samuel H. Boardman State Park. As of this writing, the trail resumes at Arch Rock Point picnic area, though plans call for development of Oregon Coast Trail sections north of Arch Rock Point in the near future. The best advice is simply to watch for an Oregon Coast Trail marker post off the highway shoulder as you approach the entrance to the park heading south on US 101.

From Arch Rock Point picnic area, about 0.7 mile south of the entrance sign for the park, the trail resumes at the south end of the parking area. It loops out along the shoreline and returns to US 101 at Spruce Island Viewpoint. The trail resumes at the parking area's south end and reemerges at the Thunder Rock Cove turnout, continuing at the south end of the turnout. It reemerges at the Natural Bridges Cove parking area and resumes at the south end of the

Opposite: *Secluded point in Boardman State Park*

parking area, on the trail to a view of the cove. Continue past the boardwalk viewpoint as the trail leads out through the woods and back to the highway. Walk just inside the guardrail to where the trail resumes under the highway crossing of Horse Prairie Creek and leads out along the shoreline and back to a highway turnout just north of Spruce Creek. Walk south inside the guardrail 0.2 mile to where the trail resumes, leading down to the beach (see North Island Trail Viewpoint–China Creek Beach Trail). Head south (rounding the point at medium or low tide) 0.4 mile to pick up the trail, which heads steeply up the bank and levels off to roll along past North Island Trail Viewpoint and reemerge at the south end of the Thomas Creek Bridge.

Cross the bridge and pick up the trail again in the parking lot just across the bridge. Follow it 8 miles through Indian Sands, along Whalehead Beach, over Sand Hill, and across Cape Ferrelo to Lone Ranch Beach (see Thomas Creek Bridge–Whalehead Beach Trail, House Rock Viewpoint–Whalehead Beach Trail, House Rock Viewpoint–Cape Ferrelo Trail, and Cape Ferrelo–Lone Ranch Beach Trail).

Section 25

Harris Beach to the California Border

The Oregon Coast Trail essentially ends at Lone Ranch Wayside. Beyond this point a combination of headlands and private land currently steers the official OCT route onto US 101 through Brookings and to the California border just south of the Winchuck River. Unofficially, follow US 101 past Harris Beach State Park and through Brookings to Pedrioli Drive, 1.5 miles south of the Chetco River bridge. Turn west on Pedrioli and follow it 0.7 mile to Ocean View Drive. Turn south and walk 1.1 miles south to the entrance to undeveloped McVay Beach Wayside. Walk west through the grassy field, bearing left to pick up the trail down the cliff to the beach. From here it's a 2.5-mile beach walk to the California border, not quite 0.5 mile south of the Winchuck River. Plan to walk it at low tide to get around the rocky promontories between McVay Beach and the Winchuck River.

Appendix I

Telephone Numbers

All numbers are within area code 503, except where indicated.

Visitors' Centers

North

Astoria Area Chamber of Commerce
325-6311

Seaside Chamber of Commerce and Visitors' Bureau
738-6391 or 800-444-6740

Cannon Beach Chamber of Commerce
436-2623

Nehalem Bay Chamber of Commerce
368-5100

Rockaway Beach Chamber of Commerce
355-8108 or 800-331-5928

Garibaldi Chamber of Commerce
322-0301

North-Central

Tillamook Chamber of Commerce
842-7525

Lincoln City Visitors' Center
994-2164 or 994-8378 or 800-452-2151

Depoe Bay Chamber of Commerce
765-2889

Central

Greater Newport Chamber of Commerce
265-8801 or 800-262-7844

Central Oregon Coast Chambers (Newport)
265-8801

Waldport Chamber of Commerce and Visitors' Center
563-2133

Yachats Chamber of Commerce
547-3530

South-Central
Florence Area Chamber of Commerce
997-3128

Lower Umpqua Chamber of Commerce (Reedsport)
271-3495 or 800-247-2155

Bay Area Chamber of Commerce (Coos Bay)
269-0215 or 800-824-8486

Charleston Information Center
888-2311 or 800-824-8486

South
Bandon Chamber of Commerce
347-9616

Port Orford Chamber of Commerce
332-8055

Gold Beach Chamber of Commerce
247-7526 or 800-525-2334

Brookings-Harbor Chamber of Commerce
469-3181

National Forest Ranger Stations

North
Hebo Ranger District
392-3161

Central
Waldport Ranger District
563-3211

Mapleton Ranger District
268-4473

South-Central
Oregon Dunes National Recreation Area (Reedsport)
271-3611

Mistix
800-280-2267

Note: Mistix makes summer reservations for five National Forest campgrounds: Sand Beach, south of Tillamook; Alder Dune, north of Florence; and Waxmyrtle, Carter Lake, and Wild Mare, in Oregon Dunes National Recreation Area.

South

Gold Beach Ranger District
247-6651

Chetco Ranger District
469-2196

State Parks

Note: Only those that accept campground reservations in summer are listed here. Call individual parks to check availability; reservations are confirmed only with receipt of a check in the mail.

State Parks Reservations Hotline
238-7488 in Portland; 800-452-5687 anywhere in Oregon

North

Fort Stevens State Park (Hammond)
861-1671

North-Central

Cape Lookout State Park (Tillamook)
842-3182

Devil's Lake State Park (Lincoln City)
994-2002

Beverly Beach State Park (Newport)
265-9278

Central

South Beach State Park (Newport)
867-4715

Beachside State Park (Waldport)
563-3220

Jesse M. Honeyman State Park (Florence)
997-3641

South-Central

Sunset Bay State Park (Charleston)
888-4902

South

Harris Beach State Park (Brookings)
469-2021

Interpretive Centers

Central

Oregon Coast Aquarium (Newport)
867-3474

Mark O. Hatfield Marine Science Center (Newport)
867-0100

Historic Alsea Bay Bridge Interpretive Center (Waldport)
563-2002

Cape Perpetua Visitors' Center (Yachats)
547-3289

South-Central

Umpqua Discovery Center (Reedsport)
271-4816

Appendix II

Recreation Index

There are opportunities for hiking and beach walking all along the Oregon coast; nearly every chapter offers suggestions for beach walks and descriptions of specific hiking trails.

To help you locate information in this book regarding other recreational pursuits, including bird watching and other wildlife viewing, use the following index.

Interpretive Centers
North 26
Central 84, 85, 95–96, 98
South-Central 133, 147

Mountain Biking and Family Cycling
North 26, 32, 42
North-Central 47
Central 88, 100–101
South 166, 176

Tidepooling
North 30, 35
North-Central 47, 52, 74–75
Central 82–83, 92–93, 100
South-Central 153, 156
South 173, 177, 187, 195, 198

Canoeing/Kayaking
North 42
North-Central 47, 59–60, 62, 72
South-Central 122–123, 133, 140, 141–143, 147
South 164

Horse Camps and Trails
North 42
Central 114
South-Central 143, 158
South 173

Bird Watching and other Wildlife Viewing
North 25, 30, 56, 105, 134, 192
North-Central 47, 49, 52, 56, 68, 70, 71, 73, 74, 105, 192, 186–197
Central 56, 58–59, 80, 82, 83, 92, 100, 112, 113, 192
South-Central 58-59, 121–122, 133, 134, 138, 147, 153–154, 158, 192
South 56, 162, 192, 196–197, 198

Appendix III

Trail Index

General Index